What they're saying about
The Telecommuter's Advisor:

". . . practical, 1990s real-world advice. . . This book is for anyone who wants to improve their remote working skills and covers a broad range of topics, including designing a home office, selecting equipment, coping with e-mail, using groupware and wireless communications, and connecting internationally." —*Booklist*

". . . a good basic guide on the subject." —*Independent Business*

"Excellent chapters on fax, modems, and voice messaging which boost the learning curve immensely. . . Extensive information on the most current computerized working issues today, such as equipping yourself to work on the road, facilitating collaboration through groupware, and attending to data security. . . a savvy and informative addition to the growing literature on telecommuting." —*Book Page*

". . . an easy-to-follow road map for working from any remote location. . . a user-friendly guide to harnessing the latest technology in order to work more efficiently and effortlessly. A 'must' for every electronic commuter in today's rapidly changing workplace." —*Midwest Book Review*

" Langhoff packs a wealth of information that's appropriately technical in nature—enough to explain in depth, but not enough to confuse the average reader. . ." —*Telecommuting Review*

"Langhoff shows how to set up a home office, including choosing the right computer, telephone, and fax systems." —*Orange County Register*

"With so many telecommunications decisions to make, you might want to read *The Telecommuter's Advisor*. . . explains what type of equipment to buy for your office as well as how to manage your fax, modem, e-mail and voice mail." —Jane Applegate, *Succeeding in Small Business* columnist

"In her books, Langhoff skillfully and simply explains how to put technology to work for you, whether you're a telecommuter, a mobile professional or a home-based entrepreneur." —*AT&T Business Network*

"Langhoff draws on almost 15 years experience as a teleworker herself to provide practical, real-world advice for anyone who wants to improve their remote working skills." —*Pacifica Tribune*

"This book will help you put the latest technology to work." —*Small Business Opportunities*

". . . provides nontechnical advice for those who work at home or from other remote locations. The book addresses issues such as setting up a remote office, choosing a voice messaging system, the use of e-mail, staying productive, and troubleshooting of potential problems." —*ISA Update*

". . . an easy-to-follow road map to working from any remote location. . . hundreds of tips on setting up a home office, picking the right phone options, coping with e-mail, managing voice-mail messages, and working on the road." —*Communication Briefings*

"Shows telecommuters how to work anywhere using the latest technology." —*Minority Business Entrepreneur*

"Being up-to-the-minute with new technologies will give you the edge you need. . . Whether you are working in an office, at home, or on the road, you will find *The Telecommuter's Advisor* beneficial to your business." —*Jackpot National Shopper Monthly*

"Telecommuting wannabes should. . . visit the (Web) pages of 'televangelist' (the teleworking kind) June Langhoff, author of *The Telecommuter's Advisor*, for sound guidance, solid info, and good humor." —*Newsweek*

"*The Telecommuter's Advisor*. . . (is) based on Langhoff's long, successful career riding the wire to work, with extensive research on the art of telecommuting in simple, nontechnical language." —*Parenting* magazine

". . . a one-stop resource for tips and information on all aspects of working away from a central office. The book is as valuable to the folks on site as it is to the ones toiling in their homes or on the road, whether for the technical how-to advice on connecting a modem and troubleshooting computer problems, or the tips on keeping interruptions to a minimum." —*PC World*

THE TELECOMMUTER'S ADVISOR

Real World Solutions for Remote Workers
2nd Edition

JUNE LANGHOFF

Aegis Publishing
796 Aquidneck Avenue
Newport, Rhode Island 02842
401-849-4200
www.aegisbooks.com

Library of Congress Catalog Card Number: 99-23768

Aegis Publishing Group, Ltd.
796 Aquidneck Avenue
Newport, RI 02842

International Standard Book Number: 1-890154-10-5

Printed in the United States of America.

10 9 8 7 6 5 4 3 2 1

Library of Congress Cataloging-in-Publication Data

Langhoff, June.
    The telecommuter's advisor : real-world solutions for remote workers / June Langhoff. — 2nd ed.
      p. cm.
    Includes bibliographical references and index.
    ISBN 1-890154-10-5 (paper)
    1. Telecommuting. 2. Home offices.   I. Title
HD2336.3L36   1999
384—dc21   99-23768
                                             CIP

Contents

Acknowledgments

THIS BOOK IS THE PRODUCT of a great teleworking team, located on both coasts. It started with a couple of telephone conversations between myself, in California, and my editor and publisher, Bob Mastin in Newport, Rhode Island. (Incidentally, Bob and I worked together for two years before meeting face-to-face.) Numerous faxes and e-messages later, we hammered out an outline and settled on a title for the book. Then Newport-based designer John Robertson took over, creating the colorful book cover and marketing materials.

Cover art, cartoons, and illustrations were done by artist Toby Dutkiewicz, based in Providence. Toby and I had a productive long-distance relationship. I'd fax or mail illustration ideas and cartoon captions to him, he'd do a fast sketch, fax it back for comments, and we'd refine the image.

Copy editor Betsy Walker, of Middletown, Rhode Island, carefully read and marked up the text in the final edit. Her inspired wordsmithing helped considerably. The manuscript was then shipped electronically to Tony Roberts in Greensboro, North Carolina, for design, layout, and copy-fitting. Tony's wife, Sherry Roberts, produced the index and proofed the final product. My best friend, designer Vicki Zimmerman, based in New York, reformatted the connector artwork to fit our page size. San Francisco-based photographer Kim Ecclesine, who I first met online, actually came to my house to take photographs for the back cover. My thanks to all of you!

A number of the true-life tales scattered throughout the book come courtesy of the members of CompuServe's Working From Home forum, where I serve as leader of the Telecommuting section. Special thanks to Kerri McBride, Steve Gallafent, Tanja Wilson, William McKee, Don Higgins, Bob Smart, Jim Hahn, Kathleen Parrish, Julie Emery, John LaBounty, Dennell Dickey, and Bill McKeehan.

Thanks also to Dave Truax, Kathie Blankenship, Art Rosenberg, Bill Holtz, Mike Irwin, Gary Hansen, George Davis, Bill Reed, Dick Knutdsen, Garry Mathiason, Ernie Vovakis, Natalie Clinton, John Girard, Eric Fecci, Ian Norman, Pete Durst, Eileen Yan, Alice Bredin, Brad Schepp, James Faraday, Mark Eppley, Mitch Kabay, and Emily Bassman.

I owe a special debt of gratitude to many of the members of the International Telework Association & Council, especially Sue Sears, Jack Nilles, Tom Miller, Gil Gordon, Joanne Pratt, Joe Licari, Diane Polutchko, Lilly Platt, David Fleming, Melissa Murphy, Harriet West, Wendell Joice, Jane Anderson, Jack Heacock, John Edwards, Michael Dziak, Margaret Klayton-Mi, Eddie Caine, Bob Fortier, and Gail Martin.

Extra special thanks to my son Nick, for cheering me up when I needed it and for playing such great background music. How many telecommuters get to write to the beat of original electronica?

I'm grateful to my pals Leonard Lucas, Annie Kook, Wootie McAdams, and Pat Rentsch for always being there for me.

Finally, special hugs for my office mates, Frisby and Marsha. I know how hard it was to keep your paws off the manuscript.

Introduction

I STARTED TELECOMMUTING IN 1982, shortly after my son was born. I had never heard the term "telecommuter." And I didn't know anyone who was working from home.

I worked for a high-tech firm in Silicon Valley—an hour's drive from my home when traffic was light. I was writing a tedious procedure manual. To reduce the time needed for rewrites, I bought a home computer—a "portable," though one wouldn't even call it a luggable now. The Osborne I, weighing in at a hefty 30 pounds, was the ultimate road warrior's machine. (Actually, it was the only portable on the market.) My Ozzie made me the envy of my coworkers, and paved the way for my ability to telecommute. Using a 300-baud external modem, I would connect to the mainframe at work and click away. It took more than five minutes just to log on. I was restricted to working in the dead of night so I wouldn't impact mainframe processing.

How times have changed! Now, millions of telecommuters work remotely from sites thousands of miles from their home, connecting over telephone lines, satellite, and cable using superfast modems. The capacity of laptops today far exceeds that of most of the mainframes of yesterday.

I still work from home, now as a full-time freelance writer. Over the years, I've learned to work effectively there and from other remote sites.

WHO NEEDS THIS BOOK?

Would you like to work from home while earning a regular paycheck? Are you interested in reducing both your commute and your stress while increasing energy and productivity? If you answered yes to these questions, read on.

This book is for people wanting to improve their remote-working skills. My goal is to provide practical, real-world advice for road warriors, distance workers, work-at-homers, and telecommuters of all kinds—from novices to masters. The emphasis is on using the latest technology to help you get work done efficiently while working anywhere you wish.

Within these pages you'll find help designing a home office, selecting equipment, coping with e-mail, understanding modems, handling fax, managing messages, maximizing your organizational and productivity skills, working with teams, using groupware, computing remotely, using wireless communications, connecting internationally, appearing in desktop video, participating in a teleconference, and working safely. There's a chapter on safeguarding your work and loads of technical tips and troubleshooting information. The appendices contain useful resources including books, magazines, newsletters, associations, online support, and more. There's a test to determine your telecommuting aptitude, tips on getting a program started, a list of organizations with telecommuting programs, and a roster of many of the jobs held by teleworkers.

I love to hear from my readers. What was useful? What was not? Suggest a topic you think should be covered in the next edition, or relate an interesting story. To contact me, send e-mail to *june.langhoff@reporters.net* or stop by my Web site (*www.langhoff.com*) and drop me a note.

I hope that my advice and the experiences of other telecommuters included in this book will help you succeed on your telecommuting journey. Happy telecommuting!

CHAPTER 1

The Telecommuter's World

WELCOME TO THE WORLD of telecommuting. Whether you've been working remotely for a few days or for many years, you're part of a major sociological trend. The move toward the anyplace, anytime workspace has transformed traditional working arrangements. Work is no longer a place. Work is simply something you do.

A LITTLE HISTORY

The first telecommuter on record was a Boston bank president, who arranged to have a phone line strung from his office to his home in Somerville, Massachusetts, back in 1877. Another early convert was John D. Rockefeller, who had workers string telegraph wire between home and office so that he could spend afternoons gardening at home but still keep in touch with the office. No one called it telecommuting then. It was just smart business.

In 1963 a programmer working on the Arpanet project (the precursor of the Internet) in Santa Monica, California, reluctantly resigned from the project. His wife was experiencing a difficult pregnancy and was confined to bed; he needed to stay at home to care for her. Art Rosenberg, a member of the project team, suggested installing an extra phone line to the programmer's house, and letting him program from there using a teletype machine. The grateful father-to-be responded by putting in marathon 18-hour workdays from home. Rosenberg reports that, "Both the project and the baby were delivered successfully and on time."

The term "telecommuting" was invented in 1973 by Jack Nilles, a rocket scientist working on NASA satellite communications projects. While stalled one morning in gridlocked traffic on the Santa Monica freeway, Nilles spotted an electronic signboard overhead used to flash traffic advisories. "MAINTAIN YOUR SPEED," the signboard advised. Nilles was going zero miles an hour. This convinced him that telecommuting had definite potential. Working with the state of California, he developed a demonstration telecommuting project. He went on to become a telecommuting evangelist, writing several books and assisting corporations in setting up telecommuting programs.

Each year, more and more people joined the ranks of telecommuters, often unofficially. Guerrilla telecommuting gained legitimacy as management saw that people working from home or from remote locations were among the most productive and loyal workers they had.

As of early 1999, about 11 percent of the workforce (nearly 16 million Americans) telecommute. In addition, about 29.3 million Americans are "day-extenders," who regularly take work home. Roughly 23 percent of the working population in the U.S. are mobile workers. Forecasters predict that there will be approximately 30 million U.S. telecommuters by the turn of the century.

A 1997 study by Olsten Corporation reported that corporate telecommuting was on the rise with 51 percent of executives surveyed indicating that their companies have a telecommuting program or a pilot underway. Public-sector telecommuting is increasing as well, especially in areas with high pollution and traffic gridlock. The federal government plans to have about 3 percent of its workforce telecommuting by the end of 2002, with a net taxpayer savings of $150 million annually. See appendix E for a list of some of the organizations with telecommuting programs.

WHO TELECOMMUTES?

All sorts of people. Their work styles range from home-based traditional telecommuting to never-in-the-office, virtual office situations. Here's a sampling:

■ Dave Truax telecommutes full time from his home outside Baltimore, Maryland, overseeing an operation spread among eight facilities nationwide. He's director of outsourcing services for Unisys. Truax keeps in touch via e-mail, daily teleconferences, and videoconferencing.

■ In Santa Monica, California, Citibank telecommuter Bob Smart took his laptop and cellular phone to the pet hospital to sit at the bedside of Chinook, his part-cocker dog, who had been nearly totaled in an automobile accident. "I sat next to her cage and typed away," he says. "Every now and then I could reach down and scratch her ears—and I didn't have to take time off to do it."

■ A group of nuclear engineers telecommute to Palo Verde Nuclear Generating Station in Tonapah, Arizona, from distances of 60 to 80 miles one way. Kathleen Parrish, their supervisor, explains that telecommuting improves their ability to respond to emergencies. "Our engineers," she says, "can get to the plant more quickly electronically than they can by car."

■ Mike Irwin is chief financial officer of Wild Planet Toys, headquartered in San Francisco. He's what you'd call a road warrior, toting his Toshiba laptop with him around the world. "My office,' says Irwin, "is wherever my computer is."

■ Jim Hahn used telecommuting to convince his employer to let him relocate from Antwerp, Belgium, to northern Virginia. Hahn coordinates international household goods forwarding. "I can live anywhere I want," he says, "as long as there are decent phone lines."

■ Carol Sparks is director of reimbursement for Summit Care, a long-term care provider, based in Burbank, California. She drives to a telework center just minutes from her home in Costa Mesa. The telecenter provides phone lines, workstations, office support services—all the comforts of the main office. As reported in the *Los Angeles Times*, Sparks saves 20 hours a week that she used to spend on clogged LA freeways.

■ Miami-based Julie Emery is a salesperson for AT&T. Her entire department has moved out of the office into a virtual office. Julie especially likes the freedom to set her own hours. "I'm a morning person and I like to be at my desk at 6:30 a.m. and work when I'm most productive."

■ Sgt. Gary Hansen of the Los Angeles Police Department, a veteran with more than 25 years of service, works at home once or twice weekly. Over the course of a year, he saves more than 4,400 commuting miles and the equivalent of almost three workweeks formerly spent on the road. Hansen reports, "I get nearly twice as much work done at home."

■ Director Steven Spielberg often edits long-distance. For example, he cut *Jurassic Park* while working in Poland on a subsequent movie, using ultra-fast phone connections over fiber-optic networks to send high-quality video and audio over great distances.

WHAT'S DRIVING TELECOMMUTING?

Increasingly, private and public organizations are adopting telecommuting as a business strategy. There are a variety of reasons: global competition, the need for 24-hour customer support, technological improvements, workers' desire for increased flexibility, and the need to reduce overhead. Jack Nilles estimates that the employee who works at home two days a week saves a company $12,000 a year. This savings results from increased productivity, reduced office space, and lower turnover.

Many companies use telecommuting as a perk to attract and retain top talent. The Dallas Museum of Art searched far and wide for the best expert on European art when it hired Dorothy Kosinski as curator, even though she continues to live in Basel, Switzerland. Long-distance relationships also

avoid the costs of relocation, estimated at around $80,000 per employee.

Telecommuting expands the radius of the labor pool. For example, Micro Focus, headquartered in Newbury, England, has several computer programmers working full time from home—one lives in Florida. Home-based work also gives organizations the ability to attract a wider range of workers including the physically challenged, parents with young children, people with eldercare responsibilities, and members of dual-career families.

Telecommuting can improve retention because employees are much less likely to leave for greener pastures. A 1997 AT&T survey of telecommuters showed that 36 percent of employees would quit or find another work-at-home job if their employer decided they could no longer work at home. A similar study by the Families and Work Institute found that 35 percent of employees with children under the age of 15 say they would change employers if they could find one that offered them more flexible work arrangements.

Telework also provides staffing flexibility. The Leisure Company, a travel reservation agency located in Phoenix, Arizona, has 50 reservation agents who telecommute full time. While the turnover rate in call centers in the greater Phoenix area hovers around 75 percent a year, turnover among those telecommuting agents averages only 5 percent annually. Operations manager Bill Reed also reports improved customer service, loyalty, and "job ownership." He further says that his employees regard telecommuting as "an indirect raise."

Home-based telecommuters continue to work at home with colds or other minor ailments that may otherwise have kept them out of the office. In fact, telecommuters work longer hours and more workdays than the average desk-bound employee. Wendy Miles, telework manager at Holland-America Westours, reports that "there were times when our telecommuters were too sick to come in to the office but were not too sick to work from home." She estimates an annual sick time reduction of about 15 hours per telecommuting employee. Diane Polutchko, director of virtual office solutions at Unisys, says that absenteeism went down 33 percent in the firm's telecommuting population.

According to the National Safety Council, stress-related problems sideline one million American workers a day. A recent study conducted at Florida International University showed that commuters needed about an hour to recover from a 30-mile, one-way drive to work. In tests administered after a commuter arrived at work, subjects gave up more quickly while performing complex tasks and were markedly more aggressive than subjects with no commute. Telecommuters avoid the stress of the daily commute and start work refreshed and ready.

Productivity often soars. Telecommuters and their managers report that workers get more done when out of the office. In an AT&T-sponsored survey of Fortune 1000 managers, 58 percent reported increased worker productivity. The State of California's Telecommuting Pilot Program resulted in productivity increases of 10 to 30 percent. American Express experienced a 20 percent gain in productivity when the company moved its on-site people to off-site call centers. Nortel experienced a 40 percent improvement in team output. U.S. West Direct found that telecommuting employees showed a 50 percent improvement in productivity during a 1997 trial.

Companies with telecommuting programs can keep going when disaster strikes. Because their road warriors tend to be widely dispersed, often a company can keep going even if the offices are destroyed. Organizations with telecommuting programs were able to get back to business within hours of the Los Angeles earthquake in January 1994. Federal employees in Oklahoma City, fearful to return to work after the bombing of the Alfred P. Murrah Federal Building in April of 1995, were permitted to work in satellite telework centers in the suburbs. Home workers armed with modems and laptops kept many eastern seaboard companies open during the blizzard of '96 and the ice storms of '98.

Environmental regulations have also encouraged many companies to find alternatives to commuting. EPA Administrator Carol Browner explains that, "If 10 percent of the nation's workforce telecommuted one day a week, we would avoid the frustration of driving 24.4 million miles, we'd breathe air with 12,963 tons less air pollution, and we'd conserve more than 1.2 million gallons of fuel each week."

According to Dee Angell, past president of the Association for Commuter Transportation, a typical commuter can save nearly two weeks a year by telecommuting one day a week.

Facility cost savings are another advantage. Dr. Franklin Becker, a professor at Cornell University and co-author of *Workplace by Design*, determined that 70 percent of desks, offices, and workstations are unoccupied during a typical workday. If workers share offices—on alternate days for example—the amount of floor space is significantly reduced. IBM borrowed from hotel designs when it consolidated 400,000 square feet of office space into a 100,000-square-foot facility at Cranford, New Jersey. Workers check in with a computerized receptionist that assigns them a cubicle and switches their calls to the appropriate cubby. This concept has saved the company $50 million annually and cut its U.S. real estate holdings by 22 million square feet.

Pacific Bell installed a "hotel" at its headquarters in San Ramon, California. The building housed 7,200 employees and was bursting at the seams. Equipping the facility with small work carrels, computer and phone hookups, and shared office equipment such as copiers and fax machines, the company could accommodate several hundred additional employees. Emily Bassman, director of virtual office development, reported that the facility, which contains 46 workstations, cost about $100,000 (they used remanufactured workstations) and saved $3.5 million the first year and $200,000 a year for the next four years in real estate costs alone.

Hewlett-Packard implemented telecommuting and virtual office programs for its sales department. Employees could decide whether they wished to stay in the office, telecommute a few days a week, or move out of the office entirely. Dick Knutdsen, Hewlet-Packard's manager of sales force productivity, explains, "We surveyed our sales force and found that the office was not a good place to get work done." He reports that sales have gone up, productivity increased, and more time is spent with the customer.

COSTS

Getting started as a telecommuter doesn't cost much. J.C. Penney provided two phone lines (one for incoming calls; the other for outgoing) as well as a PC and some other equipment for each of its telecommuting employees. Company managers found that start-up costs were less than half that of an equivalent office installation. Pacific Bell budgeted $4,000 per person per year for home office needs; Hewlett-Packard's spending ranged from $4,000 to $6,000. Many companies provide a laptop, which can be used both at the office and at home. A facilities manager at Lucent Technologies estimates that for every dollar spent setting up a home office, the company saves two dollars in real estate costs.

Not all companies foot the bill for an office at home. In a 1998 survey conducted by the Kensington Technology Group, 44 percent of employees surveyed indicated that their companies did not pay for essential work tools. But, even if you have to fund the entire expense yourself, it can still be worth it. Tom Miller, vice president of Cyber Dialogue, a New York-based research firm, explains, "You have to buy a car in order to get to work. Today, you need to buy a computer in order to work from home."

Telework consultant Gil Gordon estimates that the payback period for the technology investment to set up a virtual office is about 18 months.

Note: *For a sample cost analysis of a typical telecommuting program, see appendix C.*

TELECOMMUTING'S DARK SIDE

Telecommuting has its negative aspects as well. It's not for everybody—isolation, procrastination, even boredom get to some. Because their office can be anywhere they park their portable, workaholics often find it difficult to end their day. Temptations such as neighbors who think work-at-homers aren't really working, the lure of household chores, and family distractions can easily undermine others.

Telecommuting can cause family stress. Atlanta teleworker Dan Mendez reports that his wife resents leaving for work now that he is able to stay at home. Sherri Merl, writing in the *New York Times* (October 22, 1995), jokingly told her husband's boss that, "along with a laptop, fax, and phone line, his company should provide marriage counseling for dual-career telecommuting couples." Children can get confused, too. After working in an office for more than a year, I again started telecommuting full time. This prompted my young son to ask anxiously, "Mommy, aren't you EVER going to work again?"

Many miss the social aspects of working with other people and networking by the water cooler to keep up-to-date. Lastly, there is the real fear that telecommuters will be left out of the

loop and ignored for future promotions. Not so, says Texas-based telecommuter consultant Joanne Pratt. She discovered, in a survey of more than 17,000 telecommuters, that teleworkers receive a higher proportion of promotions than their stay-at-work counterparts (*Myths and Realities of Working at Home*, U.S. Small Business Administration, 1993).

There has been controversy over whether telework negatively affects a person's career. According to a 1995 survey by AT&T, many workers would have liked to telecommute but were afraid to. Six out of ten wannabes said they would like to telecommute but hadn't approached their bosses. They were worried that their companies might think they were less committed to hard work. However, a 1997 AT&T survey showed that more than 60 percent of survey respondents reported that teleworking has affected their career positively. Thirty-three percent of teleworkers experienced no career effect either way, while only 3 percent reported a negative impact.

When employees work outside their normal office, they increase a company's litigation risks. Garry Mathiason is a partner at Littler, Mendelson, Fastiff, Tichy & Mathiason, the country's largest employment law firm. He maintains that labor laws, written for an earlier era, are undergoing great strain. Mathiason warns that companies that rush to institute telecommuting programs without considering the legal implications are courting trouble. By focusing on potential legal problems now, they can avoid having to deal with them later in costly litigation.

Mathiason recommends that companies develop policies and procedures to address electronic workplace issues. Most employers require their teleworkers to sign a formal agreement spelling out the conditions of working at home. Ernie Vovakis, who manages a telecommuting program for California's Contra Costa County, requires a telecommuting contract. "All our people sign an agreement. To date, we've had no problems or claims."

THE FUTURE

Telecommuting and remote work of all kinds is estimated to grow at an annual rate of 18 percent through the year 2015. Free from the constraints of a nine-to-five mentality, telecommuters will continue to show high productivity—ranging 15 to 25 percent higher than what they did at the office.

Many of the personnel and legal issues raised by telecommuting will get ironed out. New laws to cover electronic workplace issues will be made covering electronic searches, workplace privacy, monitoring, network safety, ergonomics, employment discrimination, workers' compensation, and overtime.

Today you can work anywhere that has a power cord and a phone line. Batteries are getting stronger and smaller. Two-way paging and other wireless technologies continue to improve, allowing you to work untethered. Soon telecommuters will be able to sever the final ties between the office and work. Then, you'll be truly free to work anywhere anytime. Enjoy.

CHAPTER 2

Setting Up Your Home Office

HOME, SWEET OFFICE. Sounds great, doesn't it? But without some careful preplanning, your office paradise might turn into purgatory.

This chapter covers possible locations, design suggestions, and basic office furniture. We'll also discuss infrastructure issues such as power requirements and telephone wiring, and offer advice for creating a healthy work environment.

LOCATING SPACE

You need to consider several elements when determining where to locate your workplace at home. For starters, you need to find a quiet spot that is well-lit, comfortable, and reasonably out-of-the-way.

A room of your own

When I conducted my unofficial home-office survey, the item that topped everyone's list was a *door*. A door to close when the kids come home from school or when your dog decides that the mail carrier is an alien from outer space. A door for posting notices such as "Do Not Disturb" or "Hush! Teleconference in Session" is important. If you live with others (including pets), find a space that you can close off.

Some possibilities:

■ **Attic or loft**

Could be a cozy place to work. An attic, however, can become unbearably hot in summer—so make sure it's insulated and has a fan or air-conditioning. Don't plan to use it if your only access is a ladder.

■ **Converted garage**

Be sure the garage is insulated, has adequate ventilation, and natural light. Otherwise, this could be a cold and depressing workspace. If the floor is concrete and tends towards dampness, install a vapor barrier under the carpet. This provides comfort as well as safety.

■ **Basement**

Basement rooms make great workspaces if adequately lit. Be sure to get a dehumidifier if you're going to use a computer or other electronic equipment. Basement dampness could easily damage circuitry.

■ **Spare bedroom**

If you're telecommuting on a regular basis, anoint this room the official "office" and remove the bed. You'll need the space, and no one else will be tempted to invite Aunt Fanny over the night before you have a major presentation.

■ **Dining room**

This works only if everyone agrees not to eat there. You don't want to be shuffling your computer, printer, phone, and files out of the way for Sunday dinners, parties, or other major events.

Found space

If you can't find an enclosed space to hang your shingle on, don't despair. With some cooperation from your housemates, you can probably find a nook, cranny, or corner to set up a workspace. For example, you might tuck a desk and some shelves into a bedroom closet or pantry. You could appropriate a living room wall and screen it off with a shoji, pull-down shade, or drop curtain. Some people set up offices under the stairs, on a landing, along a hallway, or in the foyer.

Your corner office

If you live alone, your choices are wider. Even if you don't have an entire room to dedicate to office space, you can set up shop in a corner of the living room, dining nook, or den. Or you could raise the bed in a spare bedroom five feet by putting it on a platform, and build a mini-office beneath it. If you're going to have a miniature office, consider using portable equipment that requires little desktop real estate.

Your bedroom

You could appropriate a corner of your bedroom for your office. I operated out of my bedroom for years but don't recommend it. The office stuff tends to take over—files creep onto the bureau, the printer takes over the bedside table, office supplies sneak into your sock drawer. And then there are the incoming faxes that wake you at 5 a.m. No fun.

If you share a bedroom, it's almost impossible to work in the same space. Try making phone calls or working late when your mate is trying to sleep. It's also difficult to separate your work life from the rest of your life when you're surrounded by reminders of tasks left undone.

DESIGNING YOUR WORKSPACE

Using grid paper, plot the dimensions of your workspace. Locate the windows, doors, electrical outlets, and phone jacks. Indicate any permanent fixtures, such as overhead lights, heating vents, and closets. Next, determine your design. You have a choice of the four basic office layouts:

■ **Counter**

Line up your equipment along a worktable, desk, or countertop. This is the least ideal design for working. You'll end up doing a lot of scooting back and forth.

■ Corner

Place your desk in a corner and use a typing return, bookcase, or small stand at a 90° angle to form an L-shape. This is an efficient use of space. I work at a table made of two hollow doors cantilevered into the wall. This gives me lots of tabletop space and room underneath to store file cabinets, minitower, and office supplies.

■ Galley

This design gives you two work surfaces with space between for your desk chair. The idea is to keep your desk surface clear for writing and phone calls and to place the computer equipment on a second table or desk behind you. This is a nice design, but it requires quite a lot of room, and access is somewhat inconvenient.

■ Command center

You set up work surfaces on three sides and place yourself in the middle. Everything is within reach. This is highly efficient—and you get to feel like Captain Kirk.

You may want to draw an elevation that shows your workspace from the user's point of view and helps you determine the ergonomical placement of equipment.

Placement guidelines

■ Monitor

A notebook screen should be about 14 inches from your face. A full-page monitor should be between 18 to 24 inches from your face. If possible, position the screen so that it sits 20° lower than your eye level.

Unless you use window coverings, you'll need to place your work desk so that your computer monitor sits at a right angle to the window to avoid glare. Try to place the monitor and phone slightly to your left if you're right-handed, and to your right if you're a lefty.

■ **Computer (CPU)**

You can save space by tipping your CPU on its side and stashing it under the desk or on a bookshelf above your worktop. You might need longer power and connector cords, however.

■ **Desktop**

Standard desks are 29.5 inches high. This is great for handwriting but too high for using a keyboard. You might try an adjustable table or a separate keyboard surface placed at a lower level.

■ **Footrest**

Your feet should rest flat on the floor, and your legs should be at a 90° angle to the floor. If your feet don't reach the floor, use a footrest.

■ **Keyboard**

Typing stands are typically 26.5 inches high, but that is really too high for a keyboard. Ergonomists advise that the proper height for the keyboard is where your elbows are bent at a 90° angle and your wrists are straight, requiring a keyboard height of 23 to 25 inches. If your desk chair is adjustable, you can usually arrange to sit lower for computer work and crank up the height for writing. Otherwise, invest in an under-the-desk keyboard drawer.

■ **Power strip**

Surge suppressors and power strips generate heat. Don't place them near flammable materials such as drapes.

■ **Lamps**

Fluorescent is fine for general lighting, but use incandescent for task lighting. Place lamps and lighting fixtures to reduce shadows. If you're right-handed, place a task lamp to your left to reduce shadows. Left-handers do the reverse.

REFINING YOUR LAYOUT

Take some time to make sure that everything fits logically and conveniently. It's easy to reposition your printer or move the monitor when it's only on paper. It becomes a lot harder when you're handling the real stuff. Make paper scale cutouts of all components. Measure your cable and connectors and try out your plans on paper. To help you determine typical sizes, check the footprint chart below.

Note: *There are several software programs that support office plan design. For Windows, check out Broderbund's 3D Home Interiors, IMSI's Floor Plan Plus 3D, and Expert Software's Expert Home Design 3-D. For Macs, try Abracadata's Design Your Own Home 3D Walkaround.*

OFFICE EQUIPMENT FOOTPRINT

Equipment type	Approximate size in inches
Answering machine	6 x 9
Desk	36 x 72
External modem	6 x 9 x 2
Fax machine	16 x 18
File cabinet (2-drawer standard)	15 x 26
File cabinet (lateral)	20 x 40
Keyboard	7 x 18 up to 10 x 22
Laser printer	16 x 16
Minitower	17 x 17 x 8
Monitor (13 inch)	14 x 14
Mouse pad	8 x 11
Notebook computer	9 x 12
Personal copier	16 x 18
Task chair	24 x 24
Telephone	7 x 9
Typing return	18 x 48

OUTFITTING YOUR OFFICE

What goes in your office is controlled by what you do and what your budget is. Here are some pointers:

Seating

The most important piece of furniture in your office is your chair. Yet many home workers try to get along with castoffs. Don't. Get the best chair you can afford. Studies indicate that office workers spend 75 percent of their time seated. A poorly designed chair can cause muscle strain, backache, varicose veins, and reduced blood flow to your brain. You need comfort and support to be at your most productive.

Look for adjustable backrests and armrests, lumbar support, chair tilt, and seat height. For stability and ease of movement, get a chair with dual-wheel casters and a five-pronged base.

If you're buying a new chair, try to arrange for a trial period to be sure the chair fits both you and your work area. I didn't, and I was sorry! I found a fancy new chair, with four different controls to fit me in every way. It even had adjustable armrests that swung out and around to form computer armrests.

So I ordered it. When the chair arrived, I carted it into my office, parked it in front of my computer, and plunked down. Guess what! Though the chair had an adjustable pneumatic seat height, it lifted just an inch too short for comfortable keyboarding. And I didn't realize that ordering the swing-out arms made mine a "special order" (read nonreturnable). Dumb.

What did I do? After berating myself for a couple of weeks, I finally corrected the problem by installing a pullout keyboard drawer under the desktop.

Lighting

If possible, choose an office space with a window, preferably facing north. Natural light is great for your spirits—and your eyes. You'll probably need to add to the natural light by using track lighting or overhead fixtures. The goal is to provide comfortable light that minimizes the difference between the bright light from the computer screen and the surrounding light bouncing off walls. Use miniblinds or shades to control too much sunshine.

You'll also need task lighting, which can easily be provided with inexpensive swivel-armed architect's lamps. If your budget will allow, try halogen lighting. Halogen light is more like natural lighting and produces less glare. Although the fixtures and bulbs are more expensive, halogen bulbs last a long time (2,000 hours to 10,000 hours compared to 750 to 2,000 hours for incandescents) and are energy efficient.

Work surface

Desks are usually too small to handle all the necessary computer paraphernalia—keyboard, mouse, mouse pad, and monitor. Try to get a couple of adjustable tables instead. You want large, flat surfaces.

To reduce the possibility of eyestrain, avoid shiny finishes that reflect light. Unless you adore dusting, avoid black.

Paper handling

If you work from home only a couple of days a week, you probably won't need much space for storing files or other office stuff. But if you use your home office more frequently, you'll want a file cabinet or a rolling file to keep paperwork from burying your desktop.

Storage

At a minimum, you'll want at least one four-foot shelf for computer manuals, dictionaries, and other reference works. Bolt modular storage cubes onto the wall studs for a simple shelf system.

OFFICE INFRASTRUCTURE

It's easy to overlook such basic needs as an adequate power supply or sufficient phone jacks and power outlets, but they can make the difference between your working with ease— and hardly working.

Determining your power needs

Electricity powers your home office. Most homes and apartments are not designed with the high-tech telecommuter in mind and may not have adequate power. You may inadvertently overload circuits, a situation that poses a fire hazard. A power strip will prevent power surges, but it is no protection against overload. To find out if you have a sufficient power supply:

1. Make a list of all the electrical equipment in your office. Don't forget to include your answering machine, office radio, and overhead lights.

2. Determine the power requirements for each piece of equipment by checking the power usage chart below.

3. Add up all the amps on your list.

4. Locate the electrical panel for your home or apartment and find the circuit breaker rating (usually 15 or 20 amps per circuit, and you may have more than one circuit in the room).

5. If your maximum usage exceeds the circuit breaker rating, consult your electrician.

OFFICE POWER USAGE	
Equipment type	**Average amps**
Answering device	0.2
Color TV (13-inch)	0.7
Computer	2.0
Copy machine	12.0
Cordless phone	0.06
Fax machine	1.5
Laser printer	7.5
Overhead lights	4.5
Monitor	0.5
Modem	0.2
Radio	0.15

Example: *If you have a 15-amp rating on the circuit, and you simultaneously run electric lights (4.5 amps), a computer and monitor (2.5 amps), and a laser printer (7.5 amps), you'll exceed your limit when you turn on the fax machine (1.5 amps).*

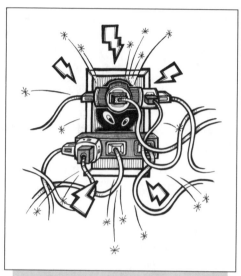

Avoid the dreaded socket octopus

Safety issues

Beware of extension cord overload. If you plug into a splitter and then plug more plugs into that before finally diving into the wall socket, you're courting danger. If too many items are plugged into the same receptacle, heat builds up. This may cause the cord's insulation to melt or become brittle. The result: exposed wires, sparks, fire.

If your socket looks like an octopus, unplug before it's too late. Arrange for additional wall receptacles or reposition your equipment so that you don't overload any wall outlets.

If you can help it, don't plan on using extension cords at all for your home office. Extensions are designed for temporary, not permanent use.

Power tips

- Copiers are power hogs. If you use one, try to put it on its own circuit.
- Use round 12-gauge wire (heavy-duty) extension cords with 3-pronged connectors.

■ Never plug electronic equipment directly into a wall jack. Use a surge suppressor (or a UPS).

■ If your lights dim when you are running a laser printer or copier, you're overloading the electrical system.

PHONE WIRING

The majority of household wiring is "twisted pair." If you cut a cross section of your telephone wire, you will find not two but four copper wires, each wrapped in a protective plastic sheath. Each wire is wrapped in a different color (usually red, green, yellow, and black).

Telephones or other communications equipment need only two of the four wires to operate. If you have only one phone line, the wires that are used are typically the red and green set. That means that you already have an extra set of phone wires in your home. To activate the second set of wires, order a new line from your phone company, connect the yellow and black wires, plug in a two-line phone and you're in business. You can do this yourself if you're handy, or hire an electrician or telephone installer if you're not.

Tips for increasing phone capabilities

■ **Use a splitter**

This lets you add a communications device (such as a fax machine or an answering machine) at the same location as your voice phone if you don't have a spare phone jack available. This device converts a single phone outlet to a multiple outlet. Splitters come in two-, three-, and even five-plug combinations and start at around $3. These devices come by many names: splitter, outlet coupler, two- and three-way jack, outlet modular adapter.

Warning: *If you put more than five devices on one phone line, you may overload the line and your phone will be unable to ring. If you need that many devices, consider getting an ISDN line (see chapter 3) or a second line.*

■ **Install a wireless phone jack**

This lets you plug a phone jack into any electrical outlet. The system comes with a base unit that you plug into a working phone jack, and an extension jack that you plug into an electrical outlet. Then you just plug your phone into the extension jack. Look for RCA, GE, Phonex, and Gennextcom wireless phone jacks at specialty phone stores (about $70 for a base unit and one extension jack, $40 for each additional extension).

■ **Get a line sharing switch**

Do you have only one phone line but want to share the line between your fax machine, answering machine, and telephone? Do you want the line to recognize the type of call coming in and route it correctly—to your phone (or answering machine if turned on) if it's a voice call, and to your fax if it hears those screechy modem tones? Install an automatic switch. If a call is made to your voice line, you can answer it or let your answering machine get it. If a fax signal is on the line, the call is automatically routed to your fax machine or fax/modem.

Some switches work with Distinctive Ringing, a telephone company-supplied service that lets you have up to four different phone numbers ring on one line (see chapter 3). Others specify which phone number should ring at each jack; still others distinguish between modem and fax calls. A less expensive solution would be to get a manual switch that lets you turn a knob and switch between two devices on a single line.

Many companies make line switches. You can also find them in mail-order catalogs:

Hello Direct (800-444-3556; *www.hello-direct.com*)

Radio Shack (800-843-7422; *www.radioshack.com*)

Electric spaghetti

The electronic age has made our work easier in many ways. Computers, modems, monitors, answering machines, fax ma-

Look familiar?

chines, feature phones, copiers, and printers are all terrific labor-saving devices—most of the time. But each device has at least one cable that you have to connect to a power supply or another device—or both. In most offices, the mess under your desk is someone else's responsibility. Not so at home. There the responsible party is *you*.

You can't just leave cords dangling, because you risk the possibility of tripping over them or stepping on them. Either way is bad news. If you step on a cord, you may break it and, even worse, if the wires end up touching, you could cause a fire.

There are several methods for dealing with cable spaghetti:

■ Bundled

Use twistems, plastic ties, or velcro cable connectors and make a neat bundle of the various cables under your desk. By looping any extra cords, you can create a relatively neat appearance.

■ Camouflaged

You can buy a flexible plastic hose and feed the cables through the hose. This substitutes one fat cord for a bunch of skinny ones.

■ Hidden

Many commercial desks and workstations come with predrilled holes (for dropping cables out of sight) and a built-in hidden cable runway. If you make your own desktop, you can easily drill holes in the top.

A HEALTHY ENVIRONMENT

Studies are underway to determine the health effects of low-level radiation, such as those emitted by computer monitors. Claims have been made that low-level radiation may cause cancer and other severe illnesses. The United States presently has no official standards for monitor emissions. Most manufacturers have adopted Sweden's monitor emission standards (MPR I & II), the toughest in the world. For the greatest safety, try to get a monitor with an MPR II rating. Alternately, you could use a radiation protection screen cover. Barring that, sit an arm's length from your monitor and sit directly in front of it (more radiation is emitted from the back and sides of your monitor than the front).

Some office equipment, especially copiers and laser printers, emit ozone, an odorless gas which may cause headaches. Many plastics used in office products give off irritating fumes. Office furniture made of particleboard, carpeting, and drapes may emit formaldehyde fumes. For safety's sake, be sure your office has plenty of ventilation. For extra security, consider nature's solution: greenery.

Nature's air conditioners

Take advantage of the natural properties of house plants to help filter the air. NASA researchers have found that some plants actually remove airborne toxins such as benzene, carbon monoxide, and formaldehyde. Among the natural air conditioners are bamboo palm, Chinese evergreen, chrysanthemum, dracaena, English ivy, mother-in-law's tongue, philodendron, pothos, Transvaal daisy, sansevieria, and spiderplant. You'll need eight to 15 plants for effective air quality improvement.

Scent sense

Did you know that certain herbal and floral scents can improve your productivity? Lemon essence, jasmine, or lavender are said to improve efficiency. Roses and tangerines reduce stress, while basil, bergamot, and cardamom sharpen your wits. Add spice to your office life with a bunch of your favorite herbs or blossoms.

Noiseproofing

Your home office will most likely be less noisy than your base office, especially if you have a door to your sanctuary at home. But the home environment can sometimes be much noisier, especially when your neighbor decides to mow his lawn right outside your office window, or the teenager down the street starts up a garage band. What to do?

Follow the advice of audio engineers and use noise-deadening materials such as drapes and carpets to absorb sound. Double-glazed windows and extra thick doors are a help. Bookcase-laden walls make great sound screens, too. A corkboard wall or wall hangings will cut down on noise as well.

A telephone headset is another good investment. Though it doesn't cut down on outside noise, you'll be able to hear better and your caller will hear less of the outside noises. For more information on headsets, see chapter 3.

If all else fails, try listening to the radio. Although it adds to the overall noise level, it can mask irritating sounds.

A FINAL REALITY CHECK

Now that you've got an office layout, show it to your family, coworkers, and boss and get their feedback. Run the numbers to determine the cost. If it surpasses your budget, trim back to something realizable. Refine the design, create a wish list for the stuff that has to wait, and finalize your plans. Then get ready to move in.

RESOURCES

Books

The Home Office Book
by Mark Alvarez
Goodwood Press, 1990
Provides real-world help finding available office space in your home, choosing furniture, buying equipment, and dealing with working solo.

The Office Equipment Adviser
by John Derrick
What to Buy For Business, 1993
A buyer's guide to help you select office equipment including copiers, fax machines, PCs, computer networks, laser printers, phone systems, voice mail, cellular, typewriters, postage meters, and shredders.

Office Design that Really Works!
by Kathleen Allen & Peter Engel
Affinity Publishing, Inc., 1995
Though this book is aimed at the small business market, many sections are still useful for home office environments.

Practical Home Office Solutions
by Marilyn Zelinsky
McGraw-Hill, 1999
Provides practical and cost-effective advice for designing an effective home office.

Design Guides: Home Office
by Sir Terrance Conran
Chapman & Hall, 1991
Conran is the most prolific designer in business today. His suggestions for small offices are creative and cost effective.

Installing Telephones
by Gerald Luecke & James B. Allen
Radio Shack, Master Publishing, Inc., 1992
Contains clear and well-illustrated instructions for making quick modular telephone replacements, adding or changing telephones, running cables, and installing single and multiline telephones.

Video

Installing Your Telephone
Radio Shack, 1994
This half-hour video covers the following topics: using modular connections, converting older wiring systems, adding a new outlet, installing round jacks, installing jacks near electrical outlets, running telephone wire, installing wall telephones, and troubleshooting.

Web sites
The following Web sites contain loads of information on ergonomic issues and provide advice on safe placement of equipment:

3M's Office Ergonomics Self-Help Site
www.mmm.com/market/omc/om_html/cws_html/selfhelp/index.html

Contains a self-evaluation tool, stretching exercises, and ergonomic guidelines.

Cornell University's Ergonomics Web
http://ergo.human.cornell.edu

Loads of news and resources for the serious ergonomics student.

CTDNews Online
www.ctdnews.com

Information on cumulative trauma injuries (CTDs) and workplace repetitive stress injuries.

CHAPTER 3

Choosing Telephone Options

OTHER THAN A COMFORTABLE PLACE to sit, the single most important item any telecommuter needs is a telephone. Since the telephone is literally your lifeline to the outside world, it is important that you use it to maximize your productivity potential. In this chapter, we'll review your home phone choices—both wired and portable. We'll examine the possibilities of using your PC as a phone, and offer suggestions on using a headset. We'll also highlight phone services that are especially useful for telecommuters. Mobile phones will be covered in chapter 9.

SHOULD YOU UPGRADE YOUR CURRENT PHONE?

You can get by with a simple single-line corded phone but, in many cases, you can improve your productivity by investing in a feature phone. If you're shopping for a new feature phone, look for:

■ **Caller ID compatibility**

Get a phone with a built-in display that shows the caller's telephone number (and sometimes, the caller's name) if the information is available. To activate this feature, you must sign up with your telephone company to get Caller

ID service (not available in all areas). Some phones also have memory capability for storing a running list of incoming caller's numbers.

■ **Mute button**

If your phone has no other features, I strongly recommend that you get a phone with this one. When you press the mute button, you can still hear your caller but your caller can't hear you. This can be a godsend when you're talking to your boss or an important client and you need to shut the office door or ask the kids to quiet down.

■ **Message waiting light**

Your phone lights a lamp to notify you if a call came in and went unanswered. This is especially useful if you have phone company voice mail.

■ **Headset-ready**

Consider getting a phone with a headset jack. That way, you can replace the handset with a headset for greater comfort and productivity. More about headsets later.

Do you need a speakerphone?

Reviews are mixed on the advantages of a speakerphone, but it's handy for winding your way through thickets of voice mail, or when you find yourself having to hold for long periods of time. It's also useful whenever you need to talk hands-free, take notes, check files, or grab a reference off the bookshelf. And, using a speakerphone definitely saves wear and tear on your neck muscles. If your current phone does not have speakerphone capability, don't buy a new phone just to add this function. Although speakerphones have advantages, they also have many limitations.

Some speakerphones use a built-in omnidirectional microphone that picks up your voice wherever you may be in relationship to the phone. However, this type of mike also picks up every other sound in the room, including the echoes your voice generates as it bounces off the walls. Many callers resent speakerphones because the echo effect is so annoying. If you want to improve your speakerphone's sound quality, use it in a room with lots of cushioning such as carpets, drapes, and books.

Many speakerphones are half-duplex. This means that only one party can talk at a time without clipping off the other person's voice. If you need speakerphone functionality for conference calling, get a phone with full-duplex capability.

How about a second phone line?

If you work from home occasionally, you can probably get along with just a single phone line. However, if you telecommute regularly, you'll need that extra line. A second phone line is absolutely essential if you plan to use your line for modem or fax purposes, or if you make a high volume of voice calls. Your business callers and coworkers must be able to reach you easily. Nor should you expect your family or housemates to stay off the home line during business hours.

The additional line also allows you to keep business calls and expenses separate from personal calling. You also want to ensure that your business calls are not interrupted by a roommate or family member picking up another extension while you are on the phone. A second line also allows you to customize the outgoing greeting on your answering machine or voice mail to accurately reflect the type of expected caller. Otherwise, you may confuse your callers with a too-formal message to your friends or an extra-casual greeting for business callers. Often, your employer will pay for your extra line.

The most common setup is to have two lines—one for your personal calls; the other for business calls. Another common situation is to have three lines—one for personal calls, one for business voice calls, and a third for data calls (fax and modem). That's what I do.

Work smart with a two-line phone

Once you have a second line, you'll probably want a simple way to manage both lines. You could place two phones on your desk and play out your fantasy of being a 1940s-type mogul, with a phone on each ear. Or you could simplify your life and invest in a two-line telephone.

I have a two-line Panasonic Easa-Phone in my home office. I use line one for incoming voice calls and line two for fax and modem calls. Occasionally, I use line two to make an outgoing call when I'm anxiously awaiting an important call. The rest of the time, I use line one for incoming and outgoing calls, and allow any overflow to go to voice mail. A line cord (called a 2-line or RJ-14 cord) runs from the phone to the wall jack and carries both telephone signals. I can take or place calls on either line and even conference two calls together at the push of a button.

Two-line phone features you'll want:

■ **Conference button**

You connect the caller on the first line with the caller on the second line by pressing the conference button. This is a useful feature—you can have a three-way conference call without paying extra for the phone service kind.

■ **Do not disturb mode**

Makes your phone busy without being off-hook. This is useful when you need an uninterrupted chunk of time to complete a project. Just make sure that your office knows when you are doing this and why. And give them an alternative method for reaching you, such as a pager or voice mail.

■ **Intercom**

This could be useful if someone in your family answers a call for you and wants to let you know about it without shouting down the hall. A far better solution is to not allow family members to answer your business line—ever.

■ **Ringer control**

You'll want to be able to selectively turn off the ringer on one or more lines, especially if you have that line backed up with voice mail or an answering device. I've turned off the ringer on my second line because my fax calls are routed automatically to my fax machine and/or fax modem, depending on which one is active.

■ Status lights

Status lights let you see which phone lines are in use. This is absolutely essential if you're sharing a line with members of the family.

GETTING CONNECTED

Modern telephone equipment uses a snap-together system of plugs and jacks to connect and disconnect devices with the telephone wiring. These connectors make it extremely easy to install or move equipment. All you do is press down on the

RJ - 11 plug

plastic locking lever and insert the plug into the jack far enough that you hear it click in place. To disconnect a device, simply press down on the plastic locking lever and gently pull the plug out of the jack.

Tips for telephone troubleshooting

■ Audio problems

If you have trouble hearing your callers, and have determined that the fault lies not with your phone, consider the possibility that you might be suffering from a slight hearing loss or be unable to hear high-frequency sounds. For around $100, you might invest in an amplified phone. This allows you to adjust the volume and tone of the earpiece.

Another alternative is to get a handset amplifier. These come in several variations. One type is plugged in between your handset cord and your handset and has a volume control dial. Another replaces the regular handset on your telephone with a special apparatus with built-in volume control.

■ Noisy lines

Static on corded phones can be caused by many things. Electrical storms, crummy wiring, and damp connectors are among the culprits. If none of these things seem to be at fault, try this old trick: Whack the mouthpiece against the palm of your hand. This shakes up the carbon granules and realigns them. High humidity can make the granules stick together, creating interference.

SAVE DESK SPACE—COMBINE PHONE & PC

If you're like most home-based workers, you suffer from a shortage of desk space. One solution is to invest in multifunctional equipment that combines two or more desktop functions into one machine. One of the most interesting multifunctional solutions is computer telephony, combining computers and telephones and sometimes a fax. You can buy software that lets you make or take a phone call, manage your phone lists, store an unlimited phone directory, autodial a number by picking it from a list on the screen, and automatically log calls. Computer telephones save valuable desktop real estate and provide greater functionality.

If you make a lot of long-distance calls, and especially overseas calls, you can save money by making them over the Internet. Users report saving 30 to 50 percent on their phone bills by using their computer to place calls over the Internet.

Web phone service comes in several flavors: PC to PC, PC to phone, and phone to phone. PC to PC service requires that both parties to the phone call have the same software and both are logged on to the Internet at the same time. PC to phone systems allows you to call anyone from your computer. To do this, you'll need to sign up with an Internet telephony service provider (ITSP). Phone to phone calling is routed through the Internet and works with a prepaid calling card.

Don't expect Internet calls to have the same high audio quality as conventional calls. Audio problems such as choppy speech, awkward pauses, and transmission delays are common. Because the voice is digitized and cut into tiny packets, it can sometimes get scrambled. Using your computer for more than one task may take too much memory away from the phone and adversely affect sound quality. Still, if you want to keep phone costs down, an Internet phone may be the way to go.

To get set up, Windows users will need a multimedia PC with a microphone, a sound card, and speakers (or a headset). Mac users that have a Macintosh PowerPC or higher are all set—the computer comes with built-in equipment for phone processing.

You'll also need software to make and manage phone calls. Here are some possibilities:

- Netspeak WebPhone *(www.netspeak.com)*

- Intel Internet Phone *(www.intel.com)*

- Third Planet Publishing DigiPhone for Mac *(www.digiphone.com)*

- VocalTec Internet Phone *(www.vocaltec.com)*

- Microsoft NetMeeting *(www.microsoft.com)*

FREE YOURSELF WITH A CORDLESS PHONE

The biggest advantage of portable phones is that, well, they're *portable*, a great boon when you're telecommuting. It's rather odd, but people assume that if you're working at home—you never take a break, go to the bathroom, or eat lunch. If their call doesn't get answered, they assume that you are just goofing off. Hardly the image you wish to project!

With a cordless phone, however, you can unchain yourself from your desk, move around, get up from your work area to answer the door, and even walk outside, and still be connected. Though earlier cordless models were noted for their poor audio quality, most models today operate at or near corded phone quality.

If you're shopping for a cordless phone, get one with multiple channels, to reduce the possibility of line interference and eavesdropping. A multiline model might be handy, if you need to field calls from more than one line. You have a choice of ranges: you can get a 46/49 MHz model, which handles ranges from 300 to 1,000 feet; a 900-MHz phone, with a range of up to ½ mile; or a 2.4 GHz model, with 20 times the range of the 46/49 and nearly eight times the range of the 900-MHz. If you're concerned about privacy, get a digital model. It's much more secure than nondigital models.

If you want the convenience of a conventional cordless phone but also want to use computer telephony, check out Microsoft's Cordless PC Phone System. The 900 MHz phone comes with software that allows you to create voice mailboxes, set the phone for Do Not Disturb (sends all your calls to your computer-based voice mail), specify which calls to ring through and which to send to voice mailboxes, dial out by using voice commands, and a number of other interesting features.

Tips for using a cordless phone

■ Privacy

If you overhear another phone conversation on your line, someone is on the same frequency channel as you. And even worse, if you can hear him, he can hear you. If you experience interference, or hear other conversations, switch channels.

If all channels are in use, you're out of luck. Cheap phones have few channels. Ten is insufficient if you work in a neighborhood with other cordless users. Higher-end cordless phones support more than 100 channels, reducing the possibility of channel contention.

■ Baby on the line

If you have a neighbor with a baby monitor, you might pick up the infant's cries over your portable. That happens because room monitors and most cordless phones operate in the same frequencies. The solution: Switch channels or get a 2.4 MHz phone, which uses a different frequency.

■ Range shrinkage

Remember, the ranges quoted by manufacturers are optimum figures. Your actual range will be considerably less because it is affected by walls, metal shelving, and interference from other electrical appliances such as PCs and fax machines.

Also, if you forget to recharge your batteries by replacing the handset, your batteries will begin to lose their power and, as they fade, the effective range of the phone will be affected.

■ Lost phone

Because a cordless phone is so portable, it's easy to leave it lying around wherever you finished your last phone call. Try to avoid this. It's not much fun hunting madly for the handset when the phone rings. Invest in a model with two-way paging. That way, you can push the paging button at the base station, causing the handset to ring, and you'll be able to track it down.

■ Broken antenna

The antenna is the most vulnerable part of your portable phone. But don't toss the phone out if the antenna breaks. You can buy an inexpensive clip-on replacement at most phone stores.

■ Mega-security

Try to get a cordless phone with a system that scrambles the voice signal, preventing electronic eavesdropping and ensuring privacy. Then if someone listens in, all he'll hear is garbled speech.

■ Power dependency

Cordless phones will not work if there is a power outage, so don't rely on a cordless as your only phone. And, because batteries tend to give out at the moment you need them most (how do they *know?*), you'll need a backup.

Troubleshooting tips

■ Make sure that your base station is located in a central location. Place it on a high shelf, far away from interference from other electrical appliances.

■ Raise the antenna on the base unit and the handset for best reception.

- Don't plug the base unit into an electrical circuit that also powers a major appliance, such as a refrigerator or microwave. If you do, you'll experience interference and may limit your range.

- Radio interference can be caused by such things as a TV, refrigerator, vacuum cleaner, computer, fax machine, fluorescent light, or electrical storm. You can do something about the electrical stuff in your office, but when Mother Nature is active, your best bet is to use a corded phone.

- If you experience noise on the line, select a different channel (or let your phone automatically search for a clear channel). If you still experience static, move closer to the base unit.

- No dial tone? Could be many things. Is the phone in standby mode? If so, select talk. Is the phone switched off? Are the batteries low? Is the telephone cord detached from the base unit? Is the base set plugged in to electrical power? Maybe the security codes in the handset and base unit got out of sync. Try placing the handset back on the base and see if that corrects the problem. After you've checked all this out, and the phone still doesn't work, it's possible that your phone line is bad. Contact your telephone repair person.

UNKINK YOUR NECK WITH A HEADSET

If you spend an hour or more a day on the phone, you may find yourself suffering from headaches or a stiff neck. The culprit may be your telephone handset. If you find yourself scrunching the phone between your ear and shoulder in order to free your hands for typing or taking notes, it's time to get a headset. Headsets come in corded and cordless models and let you take calls and work comfortably hands-free. Prices range from a low of $50 to around $200 depending on the feature set.

If you'd like to have your company buy you one, you might cite the following data to support your request:

Industry studies (H.B. Maynard & Company) show that using a headset will increase workplace efficiency and productivity by as much as 43 percent and reduce neck, shoulder, and upper back muscle tension by as much as 41 percent. If you're on the phone two hours a day, headset use will save you an additional hour and five minutes a week. Over the course of a year, it adds up to 54 hours and 16 minutes.

PRODUCTIVITY INCREASE BASED ON HEADSET USE

Time spent on phone per day	Hours saved per day	Additional calls possible per day
25%	.22	4
50%	.44	8
75%	.66	12
100%	.88	16

Source: "Do Headsets Save Money? You Bet!," *TeleProfessional*, October 1993.

Headsets replace your handset and use a modular plug to connect to an amplifier that plugs into your phone base. Your handset is connected to the amplifier as well. Make sure that your headset has a telescoping mike boom, a mute button, and a quick disconnect feature so that you can move around without having to remove it.

Expect to pay from $150 to $200 for a quality headset and amplifier. Don't economize and buy a cheap version—audio quality will suffer. Even if you don't notice it, your callers will.

Headsets require a breaking-in period. Wear your new model for short intervals and increase the wear time each day until you are handset-free (should take two to three weeks).

Unless you buy a special phone designed to work only with a headset or have a line or speakerphone button, you'll need to lift the receiver on your handset every time you make or take a call. The receiver must remain off-hook during the call and be placed back on-hook before you can receive the next call. This can get annoying real fast. To speed things up, get an off-hook device that you attach to your phone base. To make a call, you press a lever which lifts the headset. At the end of the call, just lower the lever. A really slick solution is Hello Direct's

ReadiLine (*www.hello-direct.com*). This device allows you to answer calls or hang up remotely.

If you want cordless convenience but don't like the idea of wearing a headset, there's another alternative—a phone in your ear. The Jabra EarSet (*www.jabra.com*) is a tiny, thimble-sized device that fits comfortably in your ear and replaces your telephone handset. It contains a miniature microphone that picks up only the sound of your voice. The device is connected by a cord to the 2.5mm jack on your cordless phone. Jabra also makes a model that works with your Mac or Windows computer and turns it into a hands-free telephone.

WORK SMARTER BY ADDING PHONE SERVICES

You can make your phone more productive by taking advantage of some of the services provided by your local phone company. For example, you can discover who's calling (Caller ID), arrange for several phone numbers that all ring on the same line (Distinctive Ring), or program your phone to find you anywhere (one-number service).

Some phone services require additional equipment to take advantage of a feature (such as Caller ID), but most are designed for use with a standard phone using the touch-tone keypad. Many of the features can be turned on or off by dialing a feature code—often an asterisk followed by a one- or two-digit number. If you still have a rotary phone, you'll need to prefix the codes with an 11 instead of the asterisk. Many of the codes require a *hookflash*. Depending on the type of telephone set you have, you perform a hookflash by pressing and releasing the receiver button or switch hook that sits under the handset or by pressing a flash button.

These features work on your land lines only. If you have cellular service, you'll need to check with your cellular vendor to see what is available over the air.

Make one phone line do double or triple duty with Distinctive Ringing

This service assigns multiple phone numbers to the same line. Each phone number rings with a different cadence so you can tell what type of call is ringing in—a business call, an urgent personal call (you give out a special number for emergencies), or a fax transmission, for example. Only you know that they all ring on the same line.

This service goes by many names throughout the country including RingMate, Identa Ring, Ring Master, Personalized Ring, Custom Ringing, Teen Service, Route-a-Call, Multi-Line, and Smart Ring. You pay a monthly fee per number (ranges from $4 to $7 per number)—a lot less than a separate line.

If you want to use this service to route calls to several devices such as a phone, answering machine, or fax machine, you'll need a switch with distinctive ring capability. The switch plugs into the phone line and has several modular jacks into which you plug your devices. When a call comes in, the switch "listens" to the ring pattern and connects the call to the correct device. Some answering machines and voice mail devices also support distinctive ringing. You can buy distinctive ring switches at telephone stores or computer supply houses.

Incidentally, if you have Call Waiting, it will also ring a corresponding distinctive tone (e.g., two, three, or four beeps) when a call comes in for the associated number.

You can also arrange for Distinctive Ring Selective Call Forwarding which forwards only the calls dialed. You could, for example, forward faxes to a fax mailbox, business calls to your office voice mail, and personal calls to your home answering machine if you were on the road somewhere and unavailable to take calls.

Know who's calling with Caller ID

This feature lets you see the phone number (and sometimes the caller's name) of the incoming call before you answer the phone. Caller ID is usually a combination of two features: Calling Number Delivery and Calling Name Delivery. Calling Number Delivery displays the 10-digit telephone number of an incoming call. Calling Name Delivery displays the name (as it is listed in the directory) associated with an incoming call. Both services display the date and time—a convenience especially if you are automatically logging calls.

Caller ID is useful for call screening—especially if you link it to an answering machine or voice mail. Then you can minimize interruptions, monitor calls discreetly, and decide which calls to take now, and which to return later. This capability is invaluable for telecommuters. For example, if you have Caller ID and a voice mail service, you could glance at the ID display so see who's calling, observe that it's just a chatty neighbor, and allow voice mail to pick up the call.

Another way to put Caller ID to use is to combine it with Call Waiting. Then, if you're on the phone and a call rings in and you hear the Call Waiting beep, you can check your Caller ID display to see who is calling. This let's you decide if you want to answer or stay with your current conversation. Your caller will never know the difference.

You can link Caller ID to your computer by installing software that works with Caller ID to do a "screen pop." This displays a customer's record from your database as the call comes in and allows you to be fully prepared to handle the caller's needs. Several software vendors sell Caller ID products. Some work with contact management software; others let you set up a separate database. Some possibilities:

- Call Editor from VIVE Synergies (*www.vive.com*) works with contact-management software such as Symantec's Act!

- Mitel (*www.mitel.com*) makes a computer-attached phone that provides desktop telephone controls and screen pops.

- Starfish makes Sidekick '99 (*www.starfish.com*). This well-known personal organizer program comes with Caller-ID capabilities. Requires a Caller ID interface device.

- Symantec's pcTelecommute and TalkWorks Pro (*www.symantec.com*) will capture Caller ID information and display it onscreen. Using call screening functions, you can designate certain numbers as priority and only those calls will ring through.

Using Caller ID, you can create a database of all your calls— how long each one takes, where they come from, what you talked about. Even unanswered calls are captured, so you could return them even though they didn't leave a message.

To take advantage of Caller ID, you need to sign up for the service (available in most areas) and install a Caller ID translator. This could be a phone with Caller ID display capabilities, a separate Caller ID device, or a telecommunications board installed in your computer with the appropriate software. Caller ID-equipped phones range in price from $75 to $175. If you don't need a new phone or don't want to pay those prices, you can get an add-on Caller ID display.

Caller ID information will show if the information is available. If the call comes from an area that does not allow Caller ID, the display will show "OUT OF AREA." If the caller has blocked Caller ID by using a privacy code (such as .67), you'll see "PRIVATE." If the call is coming from someone with a PBX, the number displayed will be the customer's main billing number, not the actual telephone number of the person calling.

Incidentally, Caller ID information is delivered between the first and second ring. So if you pick up too quickly, you won't receive it. Wait until after the second ring to answer.

Send your calls home with call forwarding

With a call forwarding feature, you can forward—or transfer—your incoming calls to any number you choose (even your cellular phone). When calls are forwarded, all calls ring at the forwarded-to number instead of your regular number. Use it to forward your calls from the office to home or vice versa. Send calls to a second line. Forward your fax calls to a fax mailbox when you're on the road.

When call forwarding is activated, all your calls are forwarded immediately to the number programmed. If a call comes in for you, your phone may ring about a half a ring (called a reminder ring), then the call is forwarded to the number specified. Callers won't hear a busy signal when you are on the line. However, if the number to which you are forwarding is busy, your callers will receive a busy tone at the forwarded number. You can still make outgoing calls when call forwarding is activated.

Call forwarding comes in three basic types:

■ **User-programmed call forwarding**

Gives you the ability to program your number to automatically transfer all incoming calls to another number.

■ **Busy call forwarding**

Calls forward when your telephone line is occupied.

■ **Delay call forwarding**

Calls forward when you don't answer after a predesignated number of rings. This gives you a chance to answer the telephone first.

Note: *In many areas you cannot program call forwarding remotely. Other areas offer a service that allows you to forward calls remotely by dialing an access code and personal identification number (PIN).*

If you're absentminded, call forwarding can be inconvenient. If you forget that you've forwarded your calls, your calls will continue to ring at the wrong site until someone notices and cancels the call forwarding instruction. Some smart phone systems have a reminder line or message light indicating that calls have been forwarded.

In addition to the monthly service charge, you pay normal usage charges when calls are forwarded. The charges are based on the distance from your central office to the number to which you are forwarding.

Select Call Forwarding is a similar service. This allows you to forward a list of calls to an alternate number, and to restore the line to normal operation at your discretion. You program the list yourself and can update it whenever you choose. The calling party is not aware that the call is being forwarded. Select Call Forwarding can also be used for screening calls.

If your work site is not too far from the home office, forwarding calls from the office to home makes sense. Your company would be billed for the cost of the call forwarded from office to home. If the distance from office to home could run up toll charges, arrange to have your office phone answered by voice mail, an answering device, or receptionist. It's cheaper.

Reduce costs with toll-free service

If you live a distance from your office headquarters, and phone calls to the office are billed as toll calls, you might want to arrange for toll-free access to the office. Using an 800, 888, or 877 number makes it easier to call into your main office as often as needed. All calls are charged to the company's service. And, because the company can buy toll-free service at a bulk rate, it saves money, too.

Toll-free access is also useful when you're on the road. If you travel a lot, you might want to get a personal toll-free number for calling your home office. This can save you money if you find yourself frequently calling to pick up messages or check in with the family.

Stay in touch with follow-me-anywhere service

If you are always on the go, but need to be reached easily, consider signing up for portable one-number phone service that follows you wherever you go. The telephone company issues you a new telephone number to handle all your calls. This way, you give callers just one number to call, making it simple for them to reach you, and your calls are automatically forwarded to the number (or numbers) you specify.

Ron Kopp, a management consultant, is constantly on the road. He uses a follow-me number with the ability to program three numbers that are tried serially. If there is no answer at any of the numbers specified, his calls are forwarded to his home answering machine. While the phone service is tracking Ron down, his callers hear "please stand by, we are trying your party at another location." Ron likes the ability to "give my clients, associates, family, and friends one number to use for contacting me."

Some follow-me services allow you to specify whether the caller or you is billed for the call. Others allow you to screen your callers by either listening to a voice prompt, or requiring that your callers key in their telephone number. Follow-me-anywhere service is available through AT&T, MCIWorldCom, TelePost, and several local phone services. Costs range from $1 to $9 a month, depending on the range of services selected.

A few services let you set up a schedule for call forwarding. For example, you might forward calls to your cellular phone between 8 and 9 a.m.; your main office from 9 to 5; your home phone from 6 to 10 p.m.; and to voice mail after 10 p.m. Billing can be handled two ways: Calls forwarded to you are billed to you if the caller keys in a special PIN code (which you've provided); otherwise the caller pays for the forwarding charges.

Some phone companies are offering follow-me services as a toll-free service option. You link all your messaging services—standard telephone, cellular service, fax, voice mail, and paging—to a single toll-free number. You can program a desired routing plan for incoming calls with up to three different numbers that will be tried in order. At each stage in the sequence, your caller is advised through an automated voice prompt that the system is still trying to locate you. If the call is a fax, the system recognizes the fax tones and directs the call to a fax mailbox for storage and later retrieval.

A few paging services allow you to link your own phone number to a follow-me service. This way, you don't have to reprint all your business cards and notify your callers of your new number. Some even offer an e-mail notification feature, which notifies your pager every time an e-mail message comes in.

Switch between calls with Call Waiting

This feature informs you when someone is trying to reach you while you are on the phone. While on the phone, a beep tone alerts you to another call. If you press hookflash quickly (or, in some parts of the country, key in a short code), you put the first call on hold and can speak to the incoming caller. To return to the previous caller, you just hookflash or enter the code again.

Call Waiting has its fans and its foes. Though it gives you the capability to handle two calls at once, its detractors dislike being placed on hold and are especially unwilling to remain holding during a business call. Others think Call Waiting appears tacky and low-budget. This may not be the image your company wants you to portray.

Call Waiting signals disrupt fax and modem transmissions, often causing your modem to hang up, a costly problem. If you have Call Waiting, you should get a separate line for data equipment or, at the very least, turn off Call Waiting before you initiate a fax or modem call.

Call Waiting is incompatible with the Busy Call Forwarding feature used to send calls to voice mail when you're on the phone. When your line is busy and you have phone company voice mail and Call Waiting, none of your overflow calls will reach voice mail. See chapter 7 for a complete discussion of this problem and some possible solutions.

You can cancel Call Waiting before making an outgoing call. This is usually done by pressing asterisk (star) 70 before dialing the number (1170 for rotary phone users). *Note:* This only works for the next outgoing call.

Hold a mini-conference with three-way calling

This phone service allows you to link three phone lines (two plus yours) onto one line (yours). This is great for holding small team meetings or getting an expert on the line to help you quickly solve a problem.

You can also use it to place a caller on hold, and make another call while holding the first. This lets you use it as though you had an extra outgoing line.

Tip: *If you have a two-line phone, you can simulate three-way calling by placing the first caller on hold, dialing out to the next party on line two and conferencing them together by pressing the CONF button.*

TELECOMMUTE IN THE FAST LANE

If you frequently dial into online services, connect to your office LAN, or visit the Internet, you know all about how modem speeds affect the speed that you can get work done. Many telecommuters sign up for digital phone services, such as ISDN and DSL, and alternate services, such as satellite and cable, to speed up the process.

ISDN

Integrated Services Digital Network (ISDN) is a technology that lets you turn a normal twisted-pair copper phone line into three fast digital channels (virtual phone lines). Two of the channels are 64 Kbps channels; the third, used for packet-switched transmission (short bursts of encoded information that send information such as Caller ID), ranges from 8 to 16Kbps. ISDN service lets you combine voice and data traffic on the same phone line. Use one channel as a normal voice line and the other for Internet access. Or combine the two channels for high-speed, two-way videoconferencing—all with no new wiring.

With an ISDN line connected to your PC, fax, and phone, you can send and receive just about anything—including documents, full-motion video, voice—at high speed.

Natalie Clinton, of California's Lawrence Livermore National Laboratory, reports that the labs have more than 350 telecommuters using ISDN connections. "The bandwidth ISDN provides made telecommuting feasible for many of our staff," she reports. "ISDN makes it possible for our scientists, researchers, and network managers to get the job done from home."

You'll need some special equipment to take advantage of ISDN's bandwidth. At the very least, you'll need a special modem. 3Com *(www.3com.com)* and Motorola *(www.motorola.com)* make fine ones.

ISDN prices vary significantly depending on where you live. You'll pay a one-time installation charge, a flat monthly charge, and often, a low (1¢ to 3¢) per-minute usage charge.

Although you need special equipment to take advantage of ISDN's capabilities, you can connect to any phone number. If you're using ISDN as a voice line, the called parties do not need to be ISDN-enabled nor do they have to have digital lines.

DSL

Digital subscriber line (DSL) is a digital service provided by the phone company and by some ISPs. Like ISDN, it also employs traditional copper phone lines. There are a number of DSL types, including ADSL, HDSL, IDSL, RADSL, and SDSL. Depending on the flavor of DSL you install, download speeds can be up to 1.5 megabits per second (mbps). Upload speeds top out at 384 Kbps. ADSL, one of the most common DSL offerings, is 100 times faster than 56K and 10 times faster than ISDN.

You'll need a special modem and a special card that goes inside your PC to operate DSL. You also have to be located within three miles of a telephone central office.

DSL is dedicated service. This means it connects to only one telephone number and provides always-on service. This will work fine if all you want to reach is the Net, but may be limiting if you need high-speed access to other services including your company network, videoconference sessions, or other online services.

Costs vary depending on the amount of bandwidth you order and where you're located. Service charges range from $30 to $150. Equipment will cost from $400 to $600. Installation can set you back another $100 to $200.

Satellite service

Satellite connections beam Internet data to your computer at high speeds. Speeds of up to 400 Kbps have been reported (more than three times faster than ISDN, but not as fast as DSL). The principal provider of this service is DirecPC (*www.direcpc.com*). You'll need to install a 21-inch dish antenna, a controller, and some software. You also must have a Pentium class PC, a clear line of sight to the south plus an analog modem and a phone line (to send out your request for URLs, uploading e-mail, etc.). Equipment costs about $300 plus a $50 setup fee. Monthly service rates start at $29.95 for 25 hours. Additional hours are billed at around $2/hour. If you need help installing the dish, add another $250 to the price tag.

Cable

Cable service is available through subscription to a cable data service. Speeds range from 1.5 to 3 mbps, 50 to 100 times faster than a 28.8 modem. Cable is an always-on shared service which means that as more people in your neighborhood sign on, your service will slow down. The industry leaders in cable modem service are @Home *(www.home.net)*, Media One *(www.mediaone.com)*, and Road Runner *(www.rr.com)*. You'll need to buy ($400) or lease a cable modem and a network card ($100) that goes into your computer and also run a cable to your PC. Monthly Internet access costs range between $30 and $50. Add another $100 to $175 for installation.

RESOURCES

Shopping suggestions

Consumer Reports publishes a survey of both cordless and corded telephones every few years. You can find it in your library or search it online for a fee *(www.consumereports.org)*.

Books & magazines

Phone Company Services: Working Smarter With the Right Telecom Tools
by June Langhoff
Aegis Publishing Group, 1997

Business Communication That Really Works!
by Bonnie Lund
Affinity Publishing, Inc., 1995

Computer Telephony Magazine
215-355-2866

The Phone Book: How to Get the Telephone Equipment and Service You Want—And Pay Less
by Carl Oppendahl and the Editors
of Consumer Reports Books
Consumers Union, 1991

Teleconnect Magazine
800-677-3435

The ISDN User Newsletter
Information Gatekeepers Inc., 1995
800-323-1088

Internet Telephony for Dummies
by Daniel D. Briere, Rebecca Wetzel, Danny Briere & Patrick Hurley
IDG Books, 1997

CHAPTER 4

Coping With E-mail

E-MAIL IS THE TELECOMMUTER'S GREATEST TOOL. All kinds of information can be e-mailed: memos, ad copy, artist's renderings, blueprints, spreadsheets, orders, price updates, database records, sound bites—even video clips. As a telecommuter, you'll rely on e-mail far more than your in-office brethren. Therefore, it's important that you master the necessary skills.

E-mail is more than a substitute for regular postal mail or fax because, once a message is computerized, you can copy it, store it, or forward it to someone else for handling. You can even get an electronic return receipt to let you know when someone has opened your mail.

E-mail is especially helpful for telecommuters who work across time zones or international borders. Jim Hahn telecommutes from his home in Clifton, Virginia, to his offices in Antwerp, Belgium. Hahn coordinates international household goods forwarding for Gosselin World Wide Moving and must regularly correspond with his counterparts in Azerbaijan, Armenia, Kazakhstan, and neighboring Georgia. "The only way I could get lengthy shipping documents into these countries so customs clearance could be done," says Hahn, "was via CompuServe." It was a simple download and unzipping at the other end. Instant customs approval!

Don Higgins, a full-time telecommuting systems software analyst, is a heavy user of e-mail. "As a telecommuter," Higgins says, "e-mail has become an important part of my network." Higgins telecommutes from his home in St. Petersburg, Florida, and supervises staff in Newbury, England, and Palo Alto, California. He uses two e-mail systems: his company network and CompuServe as a backup.

Use e-mail to keep in touch with the office:

- Send a weekly status report to your boss
- Remember a coworker's birthday
- Attach a spreadsheet containing this month's budget projections
- Forward an "attagirl" note you received from a client to your supervisor
- Send reminders to your team about an upcoming event

E-mail messages are *ASCII* (American Standard Code for Information Exchange) text. ASCII is the code that allows virtually all computers to talk to each other. When messages are in ASCII format, they can be sent between computers using different operating systems. This lets you communicate easily across platforms and means that people using Macs, Windows PCs, Suns—even mainframes—can read your mail and you can read theirs. E-mail works with them all.

HOW TO GET AN E-MAILBOX

If your office has a proprietary e-mail system, you will not be able to send or receive e-mail outside your organization, unless the two mail systems have a gateway. Check with your telecom administrator at work and ask if you can get modem access to your e-mail system. If a gateway exists, all you need is a home address, which you can get by signing up for a public online or e-mail service. The system you use at home doesn't have to be the same as the one at your office. For example, your office might use cc:Mail while you're hooked up to America Online.

Even if you have access to the private mail system at the office, you may wish to have a public e-mail address from an online or mail service. This gives you an alternate means of communicating and an address for nonwork-related mail from relatives, long-lost friends, and new cyberpals.

The easiest way to get an e-mail address is by signing up for one of the free e-mail services available on the Internet. Most work through a browser and require no software purchases, though you may need to download some software to make it work. Some charge extra for sending attachments. Leading free e-mail services include:

■ Juno (*www.juno.com*)

■ Net@ddress (*www.netaddress.com*)

■ HotMail (*www.hotmail.com*)

■ Yahoo Mail (*http://mail.yahoo.com*)

You could also get e-mail from an online service, such as CompuServe or America Online. Online services operate on a subscription basis, and are usually billed monthly. Most have a basic monthly service fee that will provide a minimum number of hours of online connect time and a number of services.

Note: *Be sure to find a service with a local access number so that your calls to it are billed as local calls.*

To keep costs under control, get the fastest modem you can (information about buying and installing a modem is found in chapter 5). If you can't get a local access number, check out the possibility of local Internet access through an Internet provider. Some have toll-free numbers, but their hourly rates are usually much higher than those that offer only direct dial access.

Once you've signed with a service, you'll receive a user ID and will be required to choose a secret password and, in some cases, an online identifier. I recommend that you use your own name (unless it's already taken). Your ID will appear on all your mail and forum communications and will form a part of your e-mail address. Be careful when choosing a name, as some services cannot accommodate a later change of mind. Though some people use handles like "Cat Woman" or "Bluebeard," these are obviously inappropriate for business.

IS E-MAIL RELIABLE?

E-mail is speedy. If you and the person you are mailing to are on the same mail system, it is almost instantaneous. However, if you're mailing to someone on another system, your message may take a few hours or maybe even a day to reach the intended party. Networks do not stay connected to the rest of the Internet universe all the time. Instead, they log on at intervals—every 15 minutes, once an hour, every six hours. Unfortunately, the networks do not publish their mail schedules so you have to learn their habits by trial and error.

Messages occasionally get lost in cyberspace. Even if you request a return receipt, you're still not guaranteed that your mail got through. The receipt is actually sent by the recipient's electronic post office, not by the recipient. Some mail systems can report if the message has been "read." Sounds great until you realize that a person can mark a message as "read" without reading a word.

If you send a message to an incorrect address, you'll usually get some kind of "addressee unknown" message back. Unfortunately, if the recipient has a new e-mail address, there is no facility for automatically forwarding mail. For that, you should rely on the U.S. Postal Service.

E-mail can also get stuck. So if you're used to getting frequent messages, and suddenly the steady stream dries up, don't assume that you're no longer popular or that the company reorganized and forgot to tell you. It's possible that the mail server has a problem. How to check? Ask someone to send you a message or, if you have more than one service, send yourself a message. Call the administrator or help line. I recently experienced this problem with America Online. When the mailbox was fixed, 34 messages were waiting for me (some five days old.)

PRIVACY CONCERNS

Think of your e-mail as the electronic equivalent of a postcard. Anyone who receives e-mail from you can copy it, store it, forward it to others, even edit it. In fact, e-mail you have written as an employee becomes company property. Federal law allows employers to monitor an employee's e-mail. And, if a company becomes involved in a lawsuit, discovery rules require that it produce all business records relevant to the case—including e-mail.

Even though you've deleted a message, don't assume that it is actually erased. As Monica Lewinsky and others learned during the Clinton investigations, e-mail may be archived for years as part of a routine disk backup or remain on your hard disk in an electronic afterlife. According to a new breed of computer forensic investigators, electronic mail can pile up like little ticking time bombs. *Bottom line:* avoid e-mail if you're writing something that you wouldn't want a jury to see.

E-messages transmitted over the Internet are especially vulnerable because I-net security doesn't really exist. If you need to send sensitive company information over the Internet, find out how to encrypt your file, using an encryption program such as PGP (Pretty Good Privacy) from Network Associates (*www.nai.com*).

SENDING E-MAIL

To send a message to another person, you'll need his or her address. You can look it up online (if the recipient is listed) or call and ask for it. Useful e-mail directories include:

- Any Who Directory Service (*www.anywho.com*)
- Bigfoot (*www.bigfoot.com*)
- Who Where (*www.whowhere.lycos.com*)

The address is made up of the following:

INTERNET SUFFIXES		
.com	=	business or commercial service
.edu	=	school or university
.gov	=	government agency
.mil	=	military installation
.net	=	network
.org	=	noncommercial site

Note: *E-mail addresses outside the United States often have a two-letter country code. For example,* au *for Australia,* sg *for Singapore, and* ve *for Venezuela.*

MANAGING YOUR E-MAIL

According to a 1998 Pitney Bowes survey of the communication habits of corporate and government workers, the average employee sends or receives approximately 190 messages on any given day. Keeping up with the sheer volume of messages can be a daunting task. The researchers found that the higher up the organizational ladder, the more overwhelmed the individual feels.

Unless you subscribe to an always-on service such as DSL or cable service, you must log on and check to see if you have any mail. This takes time and can run up phone charges, especially if you have to pay tolls. Alternatively, you could use an e-mail notification utility such as CheckPOP (*www.checkpop.com*) that dials your account and signals the arrival of new mail.

E-mail can pile up alarmingly fast, so if you find yourself with more than you can handle, consider getting an e-mail management program. Eudora Pro from Qualcomm (*www.eudora.com*) or Microsoft Outlook (*www.microsoft.com*) can help you screen, save, delete, or archive messages. You can create folders for various projects or clients and keep mail from overwhelming you. Workgroup software such as Microsoft's Windows for Workgroups and Lotus Notes also come with built-in mail-management capabilities.

If you have more than one e-mail address, and want to save some time, consider signing up for an e-mail forwarding service. These services allow you to forward all your e-mail accounts to a consolidated mailbox. Some services charge a small monthly fee; others are free. If you tend to change e-mail addresses often, or want to switch Internet service providers, an e-mail forwarder may be perfect for you.

Among the best-known e-mail forwarding services are:

- AmeriM@il (*www.amerimail.net*)
- Bigfoot (*www.bigfoot.com*)

- NetForward (*www.netforward.com*)
- P.O. Box (*www.pobox.com*)

STOPPING SPAM

The origin of the use of *spam* as a description for excessive e-mail came from a Monty Python show where a waiter recites the lengthy menu: "We have Spam, tomato and Spam, egg and Spam, egg, bacon and Spam" and on and on.

Junk e-mail can take over your in-box. Most large organizations have spam filters that screen out the majority of the mess, but if you use a private account to get your e-mail, you need to learn how to set up filters (sometimes called *rules*) yourself. For example, you could create rules that ignore messages with exclamation points or place all messages from your boss in your priority folder. Many e-mail software programs come with filtering utilities. Take a look at the Junk Busters Web site *(www.junkbusters.com)* for more ideas.

ATTACHING A FILE

Sometimes you'll want to send a fully formatted file to a correspondent. You do this by using your e-mail program to *attach* a file. Attached files are *binary*. This means that they aren't limited to straight text; but can contain special fonts, color, graphics, spreadsheets, artwork, software, page layouts, music, and even video.

When you and your e-mail correspondent use the same service, you can easily attach a file to the message. The attached file will retain its special formatting and arrive on the recipient's desk in the same shape as you sent it. However, if you have different e-mail services and your messages must go through a *gateway* (such as the Internet), attaching files gets trickier.

Bill McKee, an itinerant programmer teleworking his way across Australia, gave up attaching files to e-mail unless they're text only. "Not everyone I send e-mail to knows how to encode, zip, etc.," he reports, "and even those who do know how to open attached files sometimes have trouble receiving attachments." Instead McKee exchanges files with his clients over a private site on the Internet. He loads the file, notifies his correspondent by e-mail, and they download the file effortlessly.

I rarely attach files for the same reason. But, unlike McKee, I often import my file into the message, using my word processor's copy function. I lose all the special formatting capabilities, and can't send a really long file (without cutting it into smaller messages), but other than that, it works like a charm. Here's how to do it:

1. Fire up your word processor.

2. Open up the file you want to send.

3. Select the copy function and copy the entire file to your clipboard.

4. Close your word processor.

5. Start your e-mail program.

6. Select the compose mail function.

7. Position your cursor in the message body section of your message.

8. Paste in your file. That's it!

If you insist on sending attachments, make sure that the receiving party has software to unencode, unzip, and read the file. It helps if you save your files in formats that are supported by more than one platform. Here are some formats that usually work:

- EPS: Encapsulated PostScript
- GIF: graphics interchange format
- JPEG: Joint Photographic Experts Group
- RTF: rich text format (works for text files)
- PDF: portable document format (keeps formatting intact)
- Comma-delimited text: good for spreadsheets and databases

For highly sensitive mail, consider sending the document over a secure server using docSpace (*www.docspace.com*) or Posta (*www.tumbleweed.com*). These services provide file transfer and storage capabilities over the Web. Posta even produces a report showing who picked up the document and when.

OPENING ATTACHMENTS

Inevitably someone will send you an attachment that seems to be glued shut. What to do?

1. Decompress the file. If it was sent as a compressed file, it will have a file suffix like *.zip* (Windows PKZIP) or *.sit* (StuffIT for the Macintosh). You'll need corresponding software to unzip it. You can often find lite versions of these programs on the Internet.

2. Many files are sent encoded. The most common standards are *MIME, BinHex.* and *uuencode.* MIME files often have a *.mim* suffix; binhex files have the extension *.hqx* and uuencode have a *.uu* suffix. You'll need a comparable program that can decode these files.

3. Unfortunately, e-mail attachments can come with nasty infections such as the MSWord macro virus or hostile Javascript. Pass the attachment through your virus detection program such as Norton AntiVirus (*www.symantec.com*) or McAfee VirusScan (*www.nai.com*) before opening it.

4. Look at the file name suffix. This may give you a clue about what program to use to try to pry it open. If you're lucky, it's been sent in a well-supported format such as *RTF* or *PDF*. If it's RTF, most word processors can open the file. PDF files can be viewed using Adobe Acrobat Reader, available free online (*www.adobe.com*).

5. If you still can't open it, you might purchase a translator program such as Conversions Plus or Attachment Opener by DataViz (*www.datavizcom*).

E-MAIL ON THE GO

E-mail is great for road warriors, too. You can send and receive e-mail worldwide using a variety of tiny devices such as alpha pagers, palmtop organizers, and notebook computers—some wired, some wireless. When evaluating an e-mail program for remote use, be sure to consider the ability to store several dial-up access numbers.

There will be times when you find yourself needing to check your mail, but have no access to a modular phone jack. Or maybe you forgot your laptop at home. You can still pick up e-mail if you use an e-mail-to-voice program such as e-Now (*www.enow.com*) and CoolMail (*www.PlanetaryMotion.com*). Once connected to the toll-free number, you listen while a robotlike voice reads your messages back to you.

Warning: *If you sign up for a free service, be prepared to listen to some advertising messages as well.*

Note: *For more information on working on the road, check out chapter 9.*

TIPS FOR E-MAILERS

■ **Save on phone costs by composing e-mail offline**
Instead of answering mail while you're connected online, download your messages and read them after you've ended the modem session. That saves money and frees the phone line for other use.

■ **Keep line lengths to 60 characters or less**
E-mail is not like word processing. Unless absolutely everyone with whom you correspond has the same kind of computer and display as you, it's wise to limit the length of your lines to 60 characters. That way, your messages won't wrap strangely or lose the last few characters in each sentence.

■ Avoid sarcasm and irony

Sarcastic humor is difficult to convey and can easily be misconstrued.

■ Use a subject line

Most e-mail systems display a one-line summary of the messages along with the name of the sender, the subject, and the date and time sent. You can make e-messaging much easier for you and your colleagues by being as specific as you can in the subject heading. "January sales figures" is far more specific than "sales figures."

■ If you insist on using humor, make your intention clear by using emoticons

An emoticon is visual shorthand used in the online world. Here is a partial list; to view it properly, tilt your head.

:-)	smile
:-(	frown
'-)	wink
:#	my lips are sealed
{}	hug
;^)	smirk
:-\	undecided
:-$	put your money where your mouth is

■ **Don't fire off messages in anger**

If you feel like *flaming* someone, take a break, shut off your computer, and calm down. Once you've sent an angry message, you can't recall it. The damage is done.

■ **When you're answering a question, include a copy of the question**

When you answer a message, copy the original question (or the gist of it) so that your recipient knows to what you are responding. Set off the original message with carets (<< >>).

Note: *Many e-mail software programs can automatically copy the message for you.*

To: John Anybody@juno.com
From: Jane Someone
Subject: When can we meet?

<<Can you meet at the studio next Tuesday, April 7? If not, offer an alternative. >>

Hi John,

Tuesday is impossible. How about Wednesday at 3 p.m.? Let me know. And thanks!

Jane

■ **Avoid ALL CAPS**

Uppercase is the same as SHOUTING in the online world and should be avoided except for EMPHASIS.

■ **Keep it short**

Edit thyself. Your correspondents will appreciate crisp, succinct messages.

■ Proofread your message before sending

This will give you a chance to spot errors and tighten your prose.

■ Check your e-mail frequently

Most telecommuters check their mail three times a day. Follow the same time schedule that you use when you're in the office.

■ Don't let your e-mail molder

Respond to messages quickly. You'll save time if you answer at once; that way, you don't have to read the message again. If you need more time, send a quick note to your correspondent, letting him or her know that you're working on it. And, even if you're not asked for any action items, it's a good idea to let people know that you've received their message.

■ Check first before sending attachments

Check with your correspondents and ask if they can handle the attachment you propose sending. This gives them the opportunity to suggest a compatible file format or alternative (such as an *FTP* site).

■ Save time by using an address book

Keep frequent e-mail addresses in your online address book. Whenever someone sends you a message, copy the sender's online address to your electronic address book.

■ Set up distribution lists

If you regularly correspond with a particular group of people, create a distribution list and save it in your address book.

■ Avoid off-the-cuff, libelous, or incriminating remarks

Never write something you're not willing to stand behind. Remember, e-mail is not anonymous, nor is it completely private.

If you've been using office e-mail, you probably get your mail via the office LAN. At home, however, you'll need a modem. If you haven't used one before, you'll benefit by reading about modems in Chapter 5.

RESOURCES

Books

The Tightwad's Guide to Free E-mail and Other Cool Internet Stuff
by David Ebner & Henry Mullish
OnWord Press, 1997

E-Mail for Dummies
by John R. Levine (Editor)
IDG Books Worldwide, 1997

Miss Manners' Basic Training: Communication
by Judith Martin
Crown Publishing, 1996

Web sites

Everything E-Mail
www.everythingemail.net

CHAPTER 5

Managing Your Modem

WHEN I TALK TO TELECOMMUTERS, modems top their list of least favorite things. Accustomed to receiving their e-mail "magically" over the office LAN, they're now forced to hook things up themselves. And, if something goes wrong, they must try to assess the problem, and fix it themselves.

MAKE FRIENDS WITH YOUR MODEM

One of the lesser joys of working at home is learning to provide your own tech support. But you can make this task a lot less daunting by understanding the equipment you must support. Modems can be hard to use at first, but once you iron out the wrinkles, they're really very simple. Here's what you need to know:

Types of modems: size

■ **Internal modem**

An internal modem is a circuit board that occupies an expansion slot inside your computer. You must take the cover off your computer to install an internal modem. This is not difficult, but it's not for the fumble-fingered.

■ External modem

An external modem is usually about the size of a quality paperback and connects to your PC with a cable. External modems cost a bit more than internal ones, but are handier if you want to move your modem around. I prefer external modems because they have display lights that provide useful visual feedback about the status of your communication.

■ Credit card-sized external modem

If you have a notebook or handheld computer, you can get a credit card-sized modem that fits in the PC card slot (also called a *PCMCIA card*) that most portable computers have today. These tiny cards perform almost as well as full-sized modems and are easier to tote around. Of course, since they're small, they cost more.

Types of modems: functions

There are a wide variety of modems. You'll need to use the modem that is designed to perform the tasks you want.

■ Data modem

The simplest type of modem is one designed to work with *data only*. With a data modem, you can access the Internet, online services, and bulletin boards; upload and download files (including files containing graphics and sound bites); or log onto your computer at work and conduct a remote session.

■ Fax/data modem

These modems have all the capabilities of a data modem plus they allow you to send and receive faxes. To add fax capability, you must have fax software installed in your computer.

■ Voice/fax/data modem

These modems are designed to process interactive voice communications, such as audiotext, voice mail, and fax-on-demand. Some voice modems can operate as computerized answering machines.

Dual analog modem

This bonds two telephone connections together to double your speed. You'll need to find an Internet service provider that supports dual modem connections (also called multiline analog).

Although you must tie up two phone lines to get the higher speed, the equipment comes with features that allow you to share the second line with a fax or voice line. If a call is made to one of your lines, a channel can be dropped to allow the call to ring through. You could also use this type of modem to network up to four computers for a smart home network.

Radio modem

This specialized modem sends and receives data over the airwaves. Great for those of you who need to communicate in areas where phone lines are hard to find or are mostly digital.

ISDN modem

If you have an ISDN phone line at home, you'll need an ISDN-capable modem. Alternatively, you can get an adapter that allows you to attach an analog modem to your ISDN line. If you do this, however, you won't be able to take advantage of the higher speeds available with ISDN service.

Hybrid modem

A hybrid modem senses what kind of line you're using (analog or digital) and adjusts to analog or digital transmission, as needed.

DSL modem

Depending on the type of DSL service installed (ADSL, HDSL, IDSL, RADSL, and SDSL), you'll need a corresponding modem and computer card to translate the digital signals.

■ **Cable modem**

A cable modem transmits data over coaxial cable (the same stuff that carries TV signals). The modem links to the computer using the Ethernet connection on the back of your PC.

MODEM TRANSMISSION SPEEDS

Because modems and the connecting phone lines are the slowest link in your system, get the speediest modem you can afford. Modems are rated on the basis of their transmission speed, which is measured in bits per second, or bps. The most common analog modem speeds are 28.8 Kbps (kilobits per second; 1 kilobit = 1000 bits per second) and 56 Kbps.

If you were downloading a 24-page document using a modem and a standard phone line, it would take a minute and 20 seconds to transmit the document at 14.4 Kbps and 44 seconds at 28.8 Kbps. The same document would transmit in about 11 seconds over ISDN, three seconds via DSL or satellite, and less than a second via cable.

Your mileage may vary

Several elements control transmission speed including the power of your computer processor, the amount of memory and disk space available, the capability of your access equipment (modem, router, or satellite dish), the rated speed supported by your network or ISP, and network traffic—how many others are trying to move data at the same time.

Upload and download speeds vary depending on the setup you have. For example, 56 Kbps modems can download at 53 Kbps, but uploads can't go faster than 33.6 Kbps. Unfortunately, you won't always be able to operate at that speed. Many of the gateways (the modems operating at the other end of the connection) you'll encounter are geared up to handle lower speeds only. Since your modem can operate no faster than the modem at the other end of the line, your superfast modem slows down to match the gateway speed. Cable can download up to three megabits per second but uploads are poky—only 33.6 Kbps unless the cable system has been upgraded for two-way transmission. Today, the fastest uploads are available from ISDN (128 Kbps) and DSL (384 Kbps).

Also, standard phone lines are not designed for data transmission and can be full of noise and other types of interference that slow down the transmission even further. Sometimes, the dratted things hang up because the phone line is too noisy. If that happens to you, just try again. Hopefully, your connection will stay up the next time. If this happens to you often, talk to your system administrator. Maybe he or she can set you up with a digital line, cable, or satellite service (see chapter 3 for more information).

Some of the faster options require you to give up flexibility for speed. Analog modems, ISDN, and satellite service allow you to access more than one destination, whereas DSL and cable are always-on, dedicated connections and link to the same location every time. This will work fine if all you want to reach is the Net, but may be limiting if you need high-speed access to other services including you company network, videoconference sessions, or other online services.

Your bandwidth choices may also be limited by your location. Although ISDN has penetrated about 90 percent of the U.S., DSL, satellite, and cable are more limited in distribution. Even if you can arrange for a higher-speed connection, you might not be able to find a local Internet service provider or online service that can support the higher bandwidth speeds. If you do locate one, be prepared to pay a premium for faster access. Still, if your keyboard seems to be growing cobwebs between screens updates, you'll be glad you did.

COST COMPARISON

The editors of *Computer Reseller News* analyzed several of these technologies based on September 1998 prices.

COMPARING TECHNOLOGIES		
	Cost per kilobit download	Cost per kilobit upload
Cable modem	3¢	$1.49
DSL Lite	19¢	25¢
Satellite	43¢	$3.86

CONNECTING AN EXTERNAL MODEM

If you get an external modem, you'll need to plug it into your computer using either a 9-pin or 25-pin connector that plugs into the serial port on the back of your computer. If your mo-

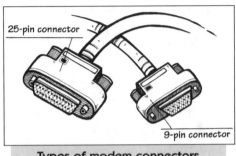

25-pin connector

9-pin connector

Types of modem connectors

dem has a 9-pin connector and your computer has a 25-pin connector (or vice versa), you can get an adapter at any computer store to make them fit. If you have a Macintosh, it's even easier to find the serial port because it's marked with a phone symbol. Actually, both phone and printer ports operate the same, so you can use them interchangeably.

Hooking up an external modem is easy. You just plug the modem into a power outlet and the phone line cord into a wall jack. Then you plug the serial connector on the modem (that's the plug with 9 or 25 gold pins) into the serial port on your computer.

DAISY-CHAINING

If you need to plug in other devices (fax machine, phone, or answering machine) at the same wall jack, you can daisy-chain them. Just plug your modem into the wall jack using the LINE port on the back of the modem. Then plug another phone line cord into the PHONE port on the back of the modem and plug in the next device. You can continue to do this with up to five devices.

TROUBLESHOOTING

Modems are simple to use. But, like any piece of electronic equipment, it helps to understand what it does, in case you need to troubleshoot a problem. Here are a few tips that may help you ride your modem to work.

Getting connected

If you have trouble getting connected, don't give up or think you are hopelessly inept. Setting up the first connection is the hardest. That's because you may need to modify your computer's preset modem instructions. You may need to add control strings (special commands) to get the connection right. Try consulting your modem manual or your company's help desk. Call customer service if you have an online service. Once you've set it up correctly, you'll be home free.

It took three different service assistants to help me set up America Online to work with a Hayes Accura 288 on my Mac. The first technician was helpful but unable to solve the problem; the second suggested a lot of control strings and finally referred the problem to the in-house tech wizard who, after a few unsuccessful attempts,

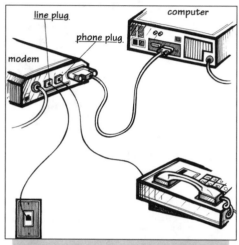

Connecting a phone and a modem with only one wall jack

solved the problem by having me temporarily remove all the *INIT* files from my system folder. Somehow, these files, which control automatic functions, were preventing the modem from dialing the 800 number.

Territorial conflicts

Sometimes a new modem won't work because it's set up for the wrong *COM* port (another name for serial port). Many PCs have two COM ports: COM1 and COM2. In addition to modems, a mouse and a scanner also require COM port space. Most communications software comes preconfigured for the first COM port (COM1) so you may have to reassign the COM

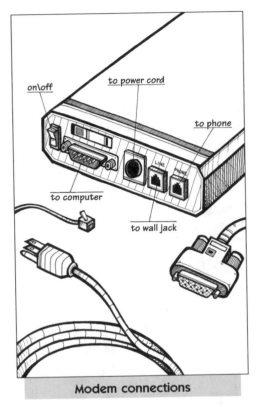

Modem connections

port to get your modem to work. There's a simple utility that lets you do this from your software; just look it up in your systems manual and follow the directions.

Protecting your modem

Modems can get hot and need air cooling to work well. Be sure that you don't block the air vents on your modem with stacks of paper or other stuff. You'll want to attach your modem to a surge protector to avoid the dangers of power spikes. Make sure the surge protector comes with a phone line connection. If you don't, a lightning strike nearby could cook your computer by traveling down the modem phone line.

Slow modem

Let's say you have a fast 56K modem and you're connected to another 56K modem. For some reason, your transmission speed drops to 46, 33.6, 28.8, 19.6, then 14.4. Finally, you're barely crawling along at 2400. What's wrong?

Nothing. Your modem connection will slow down when you have a noisy phone connection. The modems automatically adjust in order to continue the connection. The only thing you can do is hang up and try again. If you frequently encounter this problem, plan to dial at night when the phone lines are cleaner. Or get an ISDN line—digital lines are noise-free.

Modems and call waiting—a risky combination

If you have Call Waiting on the line, you're in for trouble. That's because Call Waiting tones disrupt modem communications. A Call Waiting beep can even disconnect your modem call.

You can disable Call Waiting on a call-by-call basis when you initiate a modem connection. This is usually done by dialing * (star) 70 if you have touch-tone service, or 1170 if you have rotary service.

However, if you are on the receiving end of a modem call, you have no way to stop Call Waiting from disrupting your connection. And, if you're using a remote access software program, where the distant computer dials you, you'll be in deep trouble if you keep Call Waiting service on the same line. For these reasons, I strongly recommend that you get a separate phone line for modem (and fax) communications.

Get to know what those blinkety-blink lights mean

External modems are equipped with status lights that let you know what is happening to your transmission. Many internal modems have software programs that will show the modem status lights on your screen. Get to know what the lights mean. You'll be glad you did.

One of my clients, who wishes to remain anonymous ("too embarrassed"), admitted that he only learned how to read his modem's lights after he was slapped with a $527 bill for a single modem call. Turns out the modem didn't hang up when the online software did. He didn't notice that the line was still active until the next time he wanted to dial out online, days later!

Your modem may have only four lights or as many as 12. The most common are:

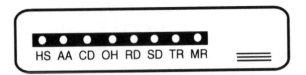

HS = High Speed
Shows that your modem is operating at its highest speed.

AA = Automatically Answer
Lights up when you have an incoming modem call. Also, if this light is on, the modem will answer your phone line.

CD = Carrier Detect
Indicates that you're connected to another modem.

OH = Off Hook
Indicates that the phone line you're using to make or receive a modem call is off-hook.

RD = Receive Data
Lights up when you are receiving data. You'll notice that this light flashes on and off in short bursts. This corresponds to the packets of information being sent over the line and is quite normal.

SD = Send Data
Blinks when you are sending data.

TR = Terminal Ready
Indicates that your computer is ready to make a call.

MR = Modem Ready
Indicates that your modem is powered on and ready to communicate with your computer.

Modem line won't release

Sometimes your modem won't hang up, even when you think it has. This may happen if your call is interrupted by Call Waiting or if your computer gets hung up and you have to reset. Be sure to check your modem line to be sure that the line has released. If it hasn't, disconnect the line from your computer and plug it back in. That should do it.

Danger: digital lines

Traveling telecommuters have an additional hazard to worry about—digital phone lines. Hotels, universities, and many larger office buildings have digital lines. If you're trying to connect your modem or other telephone device and it just doesn't act right, it's possible you've run into a digital line.

How can you tell if the phone line is digital? Look at the phone attached to the line. Somewhere on the back, you should see some text that indicates that it "complies with part 68, FCC Rules." You should also see a Ringer Equivalence Number or *REN*. If the phone has a REN number, it's analog. If no REN number appears, it's digital. Other signs of digital phones are multiple push buttons, visual displays, built-in voice mail, and keypads with special dialing or function buttons. If you're lucky, the phone will carry a warning label saying, "Not for connection to telco lines." You can also test the line (more on this below).

What can you do when you confront a digital line? The easiest solution is to request a data line—the hotel or office probably has a data line somewhere. Maybe you can borrow the fax line for a couple of minutes—fax lines are analog (unless they're Group IV fax and those lines are pretty rare). Find a pay phone with a modular connector plug; pay phones are almost universally analog. Another alternative is to carry an adapter that allows you to plug your modem line into the handset jack. Handset lines are always analog (otherwise, you'd be hearing the digital equivalent of ones and zeros). You can get such an adapter from Road Warrior Outpost (*www.warrior.com*) and TeleAdapt (*www.teleadapt.com*).

Electrocuted modem

If you suddenly find your modem not working when you plug it into an unfamiliar wall jack, you may be in for some bad news. Most PC modem cards and external modems can't take the higher electrical current that runs over digital phone lines.

If your modem encounters those lines, it burns out. That's right—dead. Kaput. Nonrepairable.

To avoid this problem, get a testing device to test the telephone port before you attach your modem. IBM makes one called the Modem Saver (*www.ibm.com*). The test is easy—you just insert the test plug in the phone jack. If it shows a green light, go ahead; a red light means danger. Incidentally, some of the newer modems have a built-in line tester.

HOW TO DIAL MANUALLY

Modems will dial automatically, but often it's easier to use your modem like a phone and dial out manually. Here's how:

1. Connect your modem to a phone line using a splitter or a duplex phone jack.

2. Connect a telephone to the phone line using the same duplex phone jack.

3. Be sure your modem software is configured for manual dialing.

4. Dial the desired telephone number.

5. When you hear the modem's squealing tones over the phone, instruct your software to connect.

6. Hang up the phone.

FOR MORE ABOUT MODEMS

If you have a fax-modem, or are interested in getting one, see chapter 6. For more information about remote modem use, and especially dialing from abroad, see chapter 9.

RESOURCES

Books

How to Connect: Driver's Ed for the Information Highway
by Chris Shipley
Ziff-Davis Press, 1993

Modems for Dummies
by Tina Rathbone
IDG Books, 1993

The Complete Modem Reference, 2nd Edition
by Gilbert Held
John Wiley & Sons, 1994

The Complete Modem Handbook
by Alfred & Emily Glossbrenner
IDG Books, 1995

The Ultimate Modem Handbook: Your Guide to Selection, Installation, Troubleshooting, and Optimization
by Cass R. Lewart
Prentice Hall Computer Books, 1997

Help lines

Contact TeleAdapt for help connecting internationally or dealing with a difficult modem. It provides assistance on its Web site (*www.teleadapt.com*) and also staffs help lines:

- United States   408-370-5105
- United Kingdom   44 (0) 181 421 4444
- Australia   61 2 9966 1744

CHAPTER 6

Handling Fax

YOU CAN'T AVOID IT: fax is everywhere. You can get your morning news via fax. You can fax an order for takeout lunch, communicate with a fax-back service to get answers to technical questions, and receive a faxed document from your teammate at the office. Although many telecommuters do not need fax capabilities, others do.

This chapter will explore the variety of options, explain fax-modem technology, and provide tips for faxing on the road and internationally. Finally, we'll compare faxing to e-mail and suggest when to use each.

A RANGE OF FAX TECHNOLOGIES

Fax comes in a wide variety, from inexpensive thermal to plain-paper laser machines that double as high-quality copiers. And, by attaching your computer to a fax modem, you can turn your PC or Mac into a send-and-receive device. You can even add portable fax capability to cellular phones and PDAs (personal digital assistants).

■ Thermal fax

A thermal fax machine uses heat to etch an image directly onto special rolls of heat-sensitive paper. Many people dislike the slick paper used; the paper tends to curl and it's hard to write on. On the plus side, thermal fax machines are inexpensive and easy to maintain. Look for one with an automatic paper cutter, document feeder, and some kind of anti-curling feature.

■ Plain-paper fax

Instead of special paper rolls, a plain-paper fax machine uses standard 8½ x 11 inch paper, the same kind used in photocopiers and laser printers. Plain-paper machines cost more than thermal fax and use one of several technologies: thermal transfer, inkjet, or laser.

■ Multifunction machine

Several manufacturers are selling combos that perform fax as well as other functions. Panasonic combines a cordless phone, send-and-receive fax capability, and answering device all rolled into one. Hewlett-Packard makes a multifunction device that combines an ink jet printer, plain-paper fax, and copier. Motorola markets a cellular phone with fax capability. The advantage: One machine does it all. The disadvantage: When your multifunction machine breaks down, you're really out of luck.

■ Fax modem

If you want plain-paper capability for less cost, and if you already have a computer and printer, consider a fax modem solution. By connecting a fax modem to your computer, and installing fax software, you can send any document that is stored on your computer and receive virtually any type of document. This saves time, paper, and hassle. Instead of printing out the document and feeding it into your fax machine, you just send it electronically from your computer. Faxes sent directly from a computer file via fax modem are much crisper than those sent from a stand-alone machine. They don't suffer any degradation from going through the scanning process. See "Using a fax modem" on the next page.

FAX SPEED

Most fax machines today are rated for 9600 bps (bits per second) or 14.4 Kbps (kilobits per second), but you may encounter older fax machines that operate at 2400 or 4800 bps. If you fax frequently, you'll need speed to keep your phone bills under control. Get a fast machine unless your faxes are all local and you don't care how long the line is tied up. Fax machines, just like modems, will slow down if they encounter noise on the phone line. Also, the transmission speed will only be as fast as the speed supported by the fax machine at the other end.

FAX RESOLUTION

The majority of fax machines let you select the quality of resolution. Standard mode is usually 100 by 200 dots per inch (dpi). Fine mode improves resolution to about 200 by 200 dpi and doubles the transmission time. Some machines also support a superfine mode (200 x 400 dpi), but they may require that the receiving fax have a superfine setting and be the same brand.

USING A FAX MODEM

The fax modem contains a standard data modem and the telephone signal processing found in a fax machine. To transmit, you use software that sends your computerized file through the fax modem to a regular fax machine or another fax modem.

When you receive a fax, the fax modem answers the call and converts the transmission into a computer graphic image. In order to receive faxes, you must leave your computer on and the fax-receive mode enabled. Leaving your computer on adds about 20¢ to your electricity bill per day. Wear and tear on your computer is minimal. Incidentally, if you're concerned about security, you'll be comforted by the fact that hackers can't get into your computer over the phone lines as long as you leave the computer in fax mode.

Incoming faxes can be viewed, discarded, printed out, or saved for later. Because you can look at them on the screen, you can delete what you don't want to print, saving time and paper. The faxes come in as graphics; you can't edit the words unless you have *optical character recognition* (OCR) capability (more about that later in this chapter).

Almost all fax software operates in the background, so you can still use your computer for other tasks. When you receive a fax, you'll be notified via a beep or a popup screen. You can either view the fax on your screen or print it out on your printer.

Advantages

Faxes sent directly from a computer file via fax modem are much crisper than those sent from a stand-alone machine. They don't suffer any degradation from going through the scanning process.

Another advantage of faxing with your computer is that you can archive incoming faxes and save them for editing, printing, or retransmission later. It's easy to create and access multiple phone books, too. You can schedule delayed faxing to take advantage of lower rates after hours. You can also efficiently send a group fax just by selecting a stored distribution list.

Of course, once you have a fax modem, you can use its data communications capability to go online, send e-mail, network on a forum, explore a BBS, or surf the Internet.

Disadvantages

If you need to send items that didn't start out as images on your computer—newspaper clippings, maps, order forms, or photos—you'll need to add a scanner to the mix. You then must scan in the image to be sent, check it for accuracy and, if necessary, rescan and finally send it as a fax. All of this takes time.

Another disadvantage is that fax files take up a large amount of disk space. A single page of faxed text is around 60K, and a graphics page is around 200K. Be sure that you have sufficient space on your hard drive to support faxing from your computer.

How to send a fax using a fax modem

Faxing from your PC is easy once you understand that your computer is being tricked into thinking that it is printing:

1. Start up your word processing software.

2. Find the file you want to send.

3. Select Print File.

4. Change your printer settings so that your fax software is the default printer. If you have a Mac, you do this with the Chooser. If you have a PC, you do this though the print command.

5. Click OK or hit Enter to indicate that you're ready to print.

6. A dialog box will pop onto the screen asking you to type the name and fax number of the person to whom you are faxing. Answer the questions and select OK.

7. The software will convert the file into a fax and then dial out. Most software will give you a report indicating success or failure.

FAX SOFTWARE

Fax modems come with bundled software. If you've purchased a new computer lately, most likely it came with built-in fax capability and a "lite" version of fax software. You aren't restricted to what came with your modem, however. You can use almost any software with a standard fax modem. So if you want additional features (such as a choice of customizable cover sheets, OCR, or fax management capabilities), you might want to purchase a more powerful fax program.

Make sure that the software supports both incoming and outgoing fax. A few of the low-cost versions only provide Send capability. Some of the best-known fax software vendors include Cheyenne Communications, Phoenix Technologies, SoftNet, Symantec, and ZSoft.

OCR explained

Some fax software packages come with optical character recognition (OCR) capability. OCR software converts incoming faxes into text files so you can edit them using your word processing program. Using OCR, you could receive a faxed document, convert it to text, port it into a word processor, mark up the file with a strike-through or highlighting font, add new text, and fax back the changes. OCR could be useful for anyone using fax for group writing projects, editorial changes, or publishing. OCR also reduces the disk space required to store a fax.

Beware: *OCR is far from perfect. Most output has errors which require careful proofreading. If you want to use OCR, be sure to coordinate with the sender, who needs to send clean, nonphotocopied documents with no illustrations, underlines, fancy typeface, or handwritten notes. Text should be in a sans serif typeface (such as Geneva or Helvetica) and be 12 points or larger.*

IS A FAX MODEM RIGHT FOR YOU?

To determine if a fax modem is appropriate for you, answer the questions below. A score of five or higher indicates that PC or Mac faxing may be the right choice for you.

- Do you already have a computer and a printer?

- Are most of the faxes you send generated from your personal computer?

- If you wish to send noncomputer-generated documents, do you have, or plan to get, a scanning device?

- Do you need to keep archived electronic copies of your incoming faxes?

- Do you want to be able to annotate faxes electronically and forward them to others within your organization or workgroup?

- Are you willing to keep your computer on all the time (or be unreachable by fax for certain periods of time)?

- Do you have sufficient room on your hard drive to accommodate hefty fax files? You'll probably want to reserve at least an additional 40 megabytes for fax storage.

SHARING A LINE

Unless you receive loads of faxes daily, you probably don't need a dedicated fax line. This means you'll need to find a way to switch between fax and voice calls. Most fax machines today come with some kind of line-sharing capability. One of the simplest involves the fax machine "listening" for a specific fax tone (called *CNG*) sent out by most fax machines. If no tones are forthcoming, the fax machine rings your phone. This can be pretty strange for callers, however, when the line is picked up and they hear nothing for up to 20 seconds. Unless they have been clued in on how to interface with your particular system, they will most likely hang up.

Not all fax machines generate CNG tones. For example, tones are not sent during manual fax calls where the person sending the fax manually dials you, waits to hear fax tones, and then presses the Send button. CNG detection is also adversely affected by noisy line conditions. No CNG tone, no fax.

A better solution is to get a fax machine with an answering machine interface. Then you plug your answering machine into the fax machine. The fax machine sits in the background, allows your answering machine to play your greeting, and listens for the incoming fax tones. If it doesn't hear anything after a few seconds, it switches the call to your answering machine. If you use this method, be sure to keep your greeting short—15 seconds or less—otherwise the sending machine will "lose patience" and hang up. Although you will hear only one ring before the answering machine picks up, your callers will hear at least three. Using this solution, your fax machine will always answer your line. The downside is that you won't be able to use your answering machine's toll-saver function.

The best choice for line sharing, if it's available in your area, is Distinctive Ring, a phone company feature that assigns multiple phone numbers to the same line. Each number rings with a different cadence so you can tell what type of call is ringing in. If your fax machine or answering device is distinctive-ring capable, it can be programmed to switch one type of ring to the fax, another to your answering machine, and so on. You could also buy a separate distinctive-ring switch that serves the same purpose. Distinctive-ring detection is highly reliable. For more details, see chapter 3.

You definitely don't want to be the human switch. I originally tried to run fax and voice over one line on my home office phone, turning on the fax machine only when I expected a fax. My callers would have to call first to arrange a fax session. Then I would unplug the phone line, crawl under the desk, plug the phone line into the fax machine, and wait. If a voice call came in, my caller would be greeted by screeching tones. This got old fast.

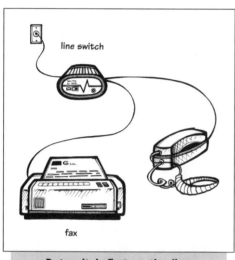

Put switch first on the line

I installed a second line to handle fax and data calls. What a relief!

GETTING CONNECTED

Hooking up a fax machine is simple. You just plug the machine into a power outlet and the phone-line cord into a wall jack. Be sure to locate yours in a secure area, away from windows, but close enough to be able to spot an incoming fax or a low paper condition.

Daisy-chaining

If you need to plug in other devices (a phone or answering machine, for example) at the same wall jack, you can daisy-chain them. Just plug your fax machine into the wall jack using the LINE port on the back of the machine. Then plug another phone-line cord into the PHONE port on the back of the machine and plug in the next device. You can continue to do this with up to five devices.

Switch first

If you're using an external line switch, just be sure that the switch is the first device on your line (closest to the wall plug) so that all devices (phone, answering machine, fax) are driven by the switch. Otherwise, the device will be unable to process calls properly.

INTERNET FAXING

Don't have a fax machine or fax modem? Or the fax machine is busy? You could send your document through an Internet-based fax service. You just download the required software (often free), attach the document you want to fax to an email message, type in the phone number and that's it.

Here are a couple of services to check out:

■ FaxStorm *(www.netcentric.com)*

■ Faxaway *(www.faxaway.com)*

■ FaxSay *(www.faxsav.com)*

FAXING ON THE ROAD

You can take fax capability with you in a variety of ways:

■ **PDA attachment**

Many palmtops and Personal Digital Assistants such as the Palm Pilot, Sharp Wizard, and Cassio Cassiopeia come with optional fax modem attachments. Some can only *send* faxes—be sure to check.

■ **PC fax modem card**

These credit-card sized devices fit in the card slot on portable, notebook, and handheld computers. You'll need a type II or III PC slot (sometimes called a PCMCIA slot) and a tiny phone jack adapter as well as fax software loaded on the portable computer.

■ **Cellular fax**

Some cellular phones have built-in fax capability. You can also get PC cellular fax modem cards.

■ **Fax-to-e-mail**

Some fax service bureaus, such as JFAX *(www.jfax.com)*, will convert your faxes to e-mail and send them on to you.

Faxing from your car

If you spend a lot of time in your car, you might consider a car fax machine. There are several options: mounted on your dashboard, wired into the car battery, or attached to your cellular phone. You can also get small, battery-powered portable fax machines to use in your car. Be sure, when shopping for a cellular fax machine, to make sure the connection is compatible with your cellular phone. There's not much standardization.

When sending or receiving, pull over and stop. Fax and modem transmissions are easily interrupted. You don't want to lose the connection when passing from one cell site to another, so stay put until the fax is through.

Connecting portable fax

Portable fax machines (other than wireless models) connect to a modular phone jack, just as desk models do. If you can't find a modular phone jack, you might want to invest in an adapter that allows you to connect to the phone's handset. Companies that sell such devices are listed in *Resources* at the end of this chapter.

Warning: Avoid cooking your modem

If you plug your modem into an unfamiliar wall jack and attempt a call, you may be in for a shock. Many hotels, universities, and larger office buildings have digital lines. Modems won't work with digital lines unless you add an expensive converter. In addition, most PC cards and many standard modems can't take the higher electrical current that runs over the phone lines of digital phone systems.

If your modem encounters those lines, it will die on the spot. To avoid this problem, buy a device to test the telephone port before you attach your modem. IBM makes one that's easy to use—you just insert the test plug in the phone jack. If the light is green, go ahead; a red light means danger. Incidentally, some of the newer PC modems have a built-in line tester. If you find your modem is in danger, you've got several options: don't fax, fax from a pay phone with a modular plug, fax from a service bureau, or use a special connector that eliminates the incompatibility.

Other options while traveling

These days, you can send a fax using a hotel's service, but you'll save money if you send it yourself. Some hotels charge as much as $5 a page for domestic outgoing faxes. The highest charge I've heard of is $10 a page in Manila.

Many road warriors use a fax service when traveling. That way, callers don't need to keep track of where you are—they just dial your fax number (usually a toll-free number) and send. You can pick up the fax at your convenience. SkyTel is the leader in this area. Prices start at around $10/month.

Online services, such as CompuServe or America Online, also provide fax options. This is how the service works: You write a normal message using your online e-mail software, log on to your online service provider, go to the Mail section, and fill in the "fax send" information. The online service converts your message into a fax and sends it on. This could save you a lot when faxing internationally.

Receiving faxes while traveling

A fax mailbox service is useful if you're out of town and still need to get those faxes. You forward your line to the fax mailbox service (using telco Call Forwarding), and it catches and stores your faxes for you electronically. You can call in to retrieve the faxes at your convenience. Fax mailbox service costs vary depending on the number of faxes received and the services you sign up for. Check out JFAX (*www.jfax.com*) and SkyTel's Fax Service (*www.skytel.com*).

Stan Ewert travels frequently and uses a fax mailbox service. He spends two weeks each month with his project team in Denver; the other two weeks he telecommutes from his home in Phoenix. Ewert combines a fax mailbox service provided by

U.S. West, with a paging service so that his faxes follow him wherever he goes. When a fax comes in, the service stores the fax and pages him. Ewert dials into the service, reviews the waiting messages, and selects those he wishes to receive. He can download faxes to a fax machine or send them to his fax modem by providing the appropriate phone number. Another useful feature is the ability to reprint a fax if it didn't come through correctly on the first pass. He also uses the fax service as a backup. "I don't have to worry about missing an important fax while online," Ewert explains. "I wouldn't be without it!"

INTERNATIONAL FAXING

If you've ever had to send a fax from Mobile to Marseilles or Newark to Nairobi, you already know that faxing across international borders can be difficult. You need a bewildering assortment of telephone prefix codes, the telephone tones don't always match U.S. tones, and telephone numbers can stretch for miles (or so it seems). If you're trying to fax back to the United States while abroad, you encounter more complexity because you have to deal with different wiring systems and network designs. Even the dial tone can be different! Here are some tips to guide you through the maze.

Sending faxes overseas

Sending a fax outside the U.S. is relatively simple, as long as you remember the following:

■ **Use international codes**

All international calls originating in the U.S. must be preceded by 011, followed by a country code as well as a city code. If you were dialing telephone number 12345 in Berlin, it would look like this:

011-49-30-12345		
011	=	**International code**
49	=	**Germany**
30	=	**Berlin**

Hint: *You'll find a list of country and city codes in the front of your telephone book.*

■ Check to see that numbers are current

Some countries are updating their dialing plans. Great Britain recently added an extra digit to the city code. Almost all city codes in the UK now begin with a 1, so you may need to add a digit. For example, London used to be 71, so now it is 171. If you were calling telephone number 123456 in London, this is what the dialing sequence would look like:

> **011-44-171-123456**

■ Change the time-out

Timing can also be an issue. Some international calls take more than a minute to complete the connection. By this time, most fax machines have lost patience and hung up. If your fax software allows you to change the time before the fax gives up, do so.

■ Get help

Telephone systems are not standardized worldwide. Therefore, your fax modem or machine may have difficulty differentiating a ring from a busy signal. This wreaks havoc with successful faxing. If you find yourself unable to get a fax through, give up and call in the experts—a fax service bureau. Send your international fax through an online service such as CompuServe.

Sending faxes from abroad

■ Teach your fax modem to ignore the dial tone

If you're using a fax modem or a portable fax machine made for the United States, you may run into difficulty when faxing from abroad. For example, the dial tone used in China is unrecognizable to modems made for the U.S. market.

If you don't change your modem to ignore the dial tone, it will patiently wait for the proper tones and never connect. So you should instruct your modem to "ignore dial tone." This lets your modem work even when it hears a foreign dial tone it does not recognize. Look in your modem's user manual and change the Detect Dial Tone setting in your setup file. Unless you adore lugging around heavy tomes, make the switch before your trip.

■ Take along the connectors you need

At last count, there were 40 different kinds of telephone jacks in use worldwide. And, even if the jack seems to fit, it still may not work because the wiring may be different. For example, British RJ-11 jacks look just like American ones but use reverse wiring.

So, if you plan to do any faxing or modeming from abroad, you've got to have the right gear. Take along the connectors you need. It's much harder to find them abroad. See *Resources* for a list of companies that make connector kits.

■ If all else fails, send your fax through e-mail

If you encounter too much difficulty sending a fax from afar, don't despair. Just switch to e-mail and let a service bureau convert it to fax.

WHEN TO USE E-MAIL INSTEAD OF FAX

If your file is already on your computer, and it's mostly text, send it via e-mail. You'll save time and money.

Example: *You want to send a 10-page fax from Los Angeles to Atlanta during normal business hours. At 9600 bps, that fax would take a little over three minutes and cost approximately $1.20. If the line was noisy and transmission dropped down to 2400 bps, the fax would take over 12 minutes and cost about $4.75. The same file, sent via e-mail, would cost no more than what you pay for the online connection. And, when the file arrived, it would be clean, readable, error-free, and computer-readable.*

Use fax transmission when you want to send information that contains complex graphics such as blueprints, photos, clippings, or handwritten notes. Use e-mail for the rest.

RESOURCES

Books

Fantastic Fax Modems

John A. McCormick

Windcrest/McGraw Hill, 1994

Helps you select, install, and customize a fax board for either your Macintosh or PC computer. Contains listings and reviews for hundreds of products.

The Totally Wired Web Toolkit: How to Use the Internet and World Wide Web as a Phone, Fax, Pager, Radio and More

by Nathan J. Muller

McGraw-Hill, 1997

The Fax Modem Source Book/Book and Disk

by Andrew Margolis

John Wiley & Sons, 1995

Connectors

TeleAdapt

408-370-5105

www.teleadapt.com

Road Warrior Outpost

800-274-4277, ext. 730

www.warrior.com

Magellan's Catalog

800-962-4943

www.magellans.com

CHAPTER 7

Managing Voice Messages

IF YOU HAVE AN OFFICE IN YOUR HOME, you need a way to cope with voice messages. After all, there will be times when you're just not available. And as a telecommuter, you've got to be accessible, or you risk being yanked unceremoniously back to the office.

There are a number of messaging options, and they boil down to two basic choices:

■ **Answering machine**

Answering machines will take incoming messages, and greet callers with an outgoing message. More expensive models will provide multiple outgoing greetings, message mailboxes, paging, and other features. Answering machines come in a variety of types, from simple tape-based answering devices to sophisticated computer-based answering systems.

■ **Voice mail**

Voice mail—a message answering and recording system provided by your paging company, telephone company, or cellular service—has the advantage of being able to take a message for you *while* you're on the phone. Thus, your callers never hear a busy signal.

ANSWERING MACHINE OPTIONS

There are a number of types to choose from:

■ **Tape-based answering machine**

If your answering needs are basic, you can get along using an inexpensive tape-based device. But steer clear of machines that use a single tape for both greeting and incoming messages. They force the caller to wait before leaving a message while the machine shuttles back to the appropriate section of the tape.

■ **Digital answering device**

Digital machines offer better message quality and faster message access. Because you don't have to wait while the cassette tape rewinds or fast-forwards, you save up to 15 seconds a message.

■ **Phone plus answering device**

Many manufacturers package a telephone along with the answering machine. Look for a cordless receiver with a built-in answering device. This allows you to screen calls from anywhere without having to be near the base unit.

■ **Computer-based answering**

Another option, if your computer has a voice-fax-modem card, is using your computer to manage your messages. Some of the latest computers come with preloaded computer phone-answering software. Some even work if your computer is off.

■ **Portable answering machine**

There are even a few portable answering machines. Motorola makes one that operates like a pager, but sends complete voice messages from your callers (*www.mot.com*).

■ **Human answering devices**

These devices, though readily available, are often highly unreliable. It's best not to expect family members or roommates to take your work-related messages. It's too easy for an important message to be overlooked or lost in the shuffle. It's a good idea to make sure that children in particular do not answer your work line. That's what voice mail is for.

SHARING A LINE

If you need to plug in other devices—such as fax machine, phone, or modem—to the same phone line as your answering machine, you can daisy-chain them. Here's what to do:

On the back of your answering machine you should find two phone jacks: one labeled LINE and one labeled PHONE. Just plug your answering machine into the wall jack using the LINE port. Then plug another phone line cord into the PHONE port on the back of the machine to attach the next device. You can string up to four additional devices on the same line.

Depending on what you connect, you may need to add a switch that can direct fax calls to the fax machine and voice calls to your answering machine. For information about fax switches, see chapter 6.

VOICE MAIL

A recent AT&T study indicates that 75 percent of calls go unanswered for a variety of reasons: The person called is either on the phone, not there, or unavailable. If you choose voice mail service provided by the phone company or other service provider, your phone will be answered automatically even when your line is busy. Overflow calls are forwarded (using standard phone company call forwarding services) to the voice mail system located at your service provider's premises. You specify when voice mail should answer your calls. It can answer when you are unable to take the call after a specified number of rings and/or if your line or lines are busy. Messages are stored on the service's computer. You call a special phone number and key in a password to pick up messages using any touch-tone phone.

The Bell operating companies, as well as numerous smaller companies in your area, offer voice mail. Prices average around $6 a month for a residential line. If you have paging or mobile phone service, ask your service provider if it offers voice mail. Many do. You might find this to be a cost-efficient alternative.

A budgetary note: *You may also be billed for calls forwarded to the voice mailbox and calls made to pick up messages (depending on your particular type of phone service and the distance of the call). This can add up, especially if your assigned voice mail machine is not located within your low-cost calling area and you rack up toll charges every time a call is forwarded to voice mail. Best to ask before you sign up.*

I've had voice mail service for many years. I pay the residential rate, which in California is less than $7 a month. Because I have a special rate plan that allows unlimited calls in my local calling area, I pay nothing extra for forwarding calls to voice mail. And, as long as I call in for messages from a local phone, I pay nothing extra to access my calls. Though the monthly fee is cheap, over the years it does add up. Yet I'm still happy with my choice because, for that price, I get virtually unlimited incoming message service.

I also like the messaging function, which lets me send and receive messages to voice mail subscribers throughout northern California without having to place a phone call. I have one workaholic editor who used to call me at 5:30 a.m. Since I work out of my home, this became quite an intrusion. Now she drops a message in my mailbox which I can access when I awake—at a more civilized hour.

Add a visual message-waiting lamp

Some people dislike having to pick up the handset and listen for the message-waiting tone to check for messages. You can get a nifty little device that clips onto your phone line to notify you that messages are waiting. Two to check out are the Voice Mail Message Light from SoloPoint *(www.solopoint.com)* and the VisuAlert from Palco Telecom *(www.palcotel.com)*.

Screen your voice-mail calls

A major complaint of some voice mail users is the lack of ability to screen calls, something easy to do with an answering machine. SoloPoint has a solution. It developed the Voice Mail Enhancer, which you attach to your phone line. This small device provides a visual message waiting indicator, allows you to listen in on callers leaving messages with your voice mail service, provides the capability to break into the message and take over the call, and even lets you connect a fax machine to your voice mail line. You'll need to sign up for three-way calling service to operate the device. An enhanced version of the product includes Caller ID and PC call-logging capability.

"To hear the latest corporate rumors, press two; to find out who just got laid off, press three; to check on the status of your job, press..."

Keep in touch with voice mail

Voice mail and Call Waiting

Beware: The tones generated by Call Waiting notification may play havoc with your voice mail setup if voice mail is programmed to pick up your calls when your phone line is busy. That's because Call Waiting and busy call forwarding are in conflict. The former tells your phone switch to alert you if a call is coming in while you're on the phone. The latter tells your phone switch to bypass you and send the call to the forwarded number. Phone systems have decision trees that tell them which function takes precedence if and when they get conflicting instructions. In this case, Call Waiting will override the busy call forwarding feature. This means that none of your overflow calls will reach voice mail when you're on the line.

Note: *Phone companies are addressing this problem and are developing technology to correct it. Check with your voice mail provider to see if it can offer additional suggestions.*

If you have Call Waiting and phone company voice mail with the Busy Call Forwarding feature, you have three options:

■ **Cancel Call Waiting before every outgoing call**

Temporarily turn off Call Waiting before making an outbound call so you won't be interrupted during the call. You do this by dialing *(star) 70 (available in most central office switches). Call Waiting is canceled only for the duration of that one outgoing call. Incoming calls will forward to voice mail.

If you're willing to punch in the code before every call, this will take care of calls coming in while you're making an outgoing call, but it still won't help you when you've answered an incoming call and another call comes in.

■ **Remove Call Waiting**

Call your phone company and tell them to remove Call Waiting from your line. You don't really need it now that you have the ability to get a message from every incoming caller. This will save money, too.

■ **Remove Busy Call Forwarding**

If you can't part with Call Waiting, ask your phone company to remove the busy call forwarding feature. You can't really take advantage of it anyway if you have Call Waiting. Depending on how the pricing is bundled, you might save some money.

WHAT'S BEST FOR YOU?

One thing we all know for sure—you need some kind of messaging capability. Now what kind will you use?

Telephone answering machines (TAMs) are very flexible. You are in control of the programming. You can see at a glance that you have messages, and you don't have to place a phone call to pick them up. TAMs are usually less expensive than voice mail. Though you pay the up-front cost of buying the answering equipment, there are no monthly fees. TAMs let you easily monitor incoming calls, which is helpful if you want to get some work done while waiting for that all-important call. If you need to keep audio records, it's easy to archive messages—although you might get sick of a filing cabinet overflowing with cassette tapes.

Voice mail's biggest advantage is that it takes messages even when you're on the phone, so your callers don't have to hear a busy signal. Message handling on voice mail is more functional—especially the broadcasting and messaging capabilities. A message on an answering device is just that—you can listen to it, save it, or erase it, but you can't send it to another user, add comments, or port it to your PC for later reference.

TAMs are still not the most reliable devices. The moving parts sometimes malfunction. Power availability can be a problem. If you live in an area that suffers from brownouts and electrical failures, an answering machine may not be reliable enough.

However, if you need to speak to your callers real-time the first time they call, voice mail is no improvement over an answering machine. You'd be better off with a mobile phone or a follow-me-anywhere phone number.

SETTING UP YOUR MESSAGING SYSTEM

The key to an effective message system is to keep your caller in mind at all times. Think about how you feel when someone doesn't return your calls promptly. Be sure to avoid using voice mail or an answering device as a shield to keep callers at a distance. The following tips will help you tune up your voice communications.

■ **Encourage callers to leave details**

A message that consists of just a name and number is not helpful because you have to call back just to find out what the caller needs. Suggest that your callers ask their questions now and, if they have one-way information, to leave it. A friend of mine adds this tagline to the end of his message:

> **If you leave me a detailed message, I'll be able to get back to you with the information you need.**

■ Provide alternate ways to reach you

When I'm conducting many interviews by phone, or trying to round up lots of information, I include my fax number in the message. That way, the person returning my call doesn't have to connect with me personally. It saves time for both of us.

> **Hello. You've reached June Langhoff's voice mail. I'm in the office today but am on the phone right now. If you have a press release to send me, my fax number is 650-555-3456. Otherwise, leave me a message and I'll get back to you promptly.**

■ Keep your greeting short and businesslike

Although some people may enjoy a good joke or your comments about last night's news, the majority of your callers will be irritated or even offended.

■ Speak in a natural tone

When recording, never *read* your greeting. You'll sound nervous or aloof. Rehearse your outgoing message until you sound natural, relaxed, and upbeat.

■ Provide instructions for emergencies

If your callers need help fast, give them an option. This could be pressing a key combination to label the call urgent, indicating that all or urgent calls ring your pager, or providing an alternate number to call.

> **This is Alex Hamilton's voice mail. Please leave your name, number, and a detailed message and I'll get back to you as quickly as I can. If you need help immediately, press the four key after you leave your message and I will be paged.**

■ Change your outgoing message frequently

Your greeting should let callers know whether you are just briefly away from the phone or gone for a few days. The purpose is twofold: You're giving the caller an idea of how soon you'll return his or her call (two hours, end of day, next week), and your frequent caller will know that you use voice mail actively. Some people even put the day's date in their greeting.

> You've reached Aaron Burr at Acme Consultants. It's Tuesday, August 14th. I'll be in meetings this morning but will be checking for messages. This afternoon, I'll be in the office.

■ Keep tabs on your sound quality

Call yourself and leave messages periodically to check how you sound.

■ Pay close attention to the audio

If you have potentially distracting background sounds, close the door or wait until it's quiet to change your greeting. Whatever you do, don't use a speakerphone when recording your greeting—unless you want to sound imperious and distant.

■ Check in regularly

This simplifies the task of returning calls and lets you respond quickly to important or urgent calls. Be sure to avoid all possible appearance of hiding behind your voice mail or answering machine.

■ Provide shortcut tips for regular callers

I really appreciate greetings that recognize that frequent callers may hear the same informational message over and over—and over—again. So, tell your callers how to skip your greeting and get right to the message-leaving part. Voice mail and some answering machines provide this function.

> **If you would like to skip this message and leave a message for me, press the pound sign now.**

■ **Pack a pager**

If you don't want to provide your home office number over voice mail or on the answering machine, arrange for a paging service to contact you. This is also useful when you travel frequently and are at different locations throughout the day.

TIPS FOR EFFECTIVE MESSAGES

On the days that you work from home, you'll rely on the phone a great deal. And that means that you'll have to leave messages for customers and coworkers more often than you will on your in-office days. Here are some tips to help you leave the kind of message that will reduce telephone tag and increase the odds that your call will be returned.

■ **Organize before calling**

Be brief and to-the-point. Skip the small talk. If you need a response, include a good time to reach you and how urgent your need is.

■ **Identify yourself immediately**

Most voice mail systems and some answering machines have a scanning feature that allows the recipient to play only the first few seconds of the message. You want to let the recipient know who's calling up front.

■ **Headline your message**

Explain the subject of your message. This helps the recipient decide whether to listen to the message now or save it for later.

■ **Save your telephone number for last**

Most voice systems allow users to skip to the last 10 seconds of the message because the majority leave their phone number last.

■ **Always provide your phone number**

This saves the recipient time because he or she doesn't have to look your number up. It also increases your chances of a callback if the recipient is out of the office and does not have access to a phone book or Rolodex.

■ **Slow down when leaving numbers**

Doesn't it drive you nuts when someone leaves you a perfectly clear message and then races through the phone number at the end so you have to play the message over and over to get it right? So, even though you are totally bored with repeating your phone number, resist the temptation to hurry through this part.

RESOURCES

Shopping suggestions

Consumer Reports publishes a survey of answering machines every few years. You can find it in your library or search it online for a fee *(www.consumereports.org)*.

Books

1-800 Courtesy:
Connecting With A Winning Telephone Image
by Terry Wildermann
Aegis Publishing, 1999
Not just another telephone etiquette book, this one offers useful tips on managing your phone and working effectively from home.

CHAPTER 8

Staying Productive

YOU'RE AN ORGANIZED PERSON, right? So you're just going to skip this chapter, right again? Wrong!

Even though you are super productive at the office, you'll face a whole new set of challenges at home. Though you know how to successfully circumvent the office bore and sidestep the water-cooler crowd, you might not know how to avoid such domestic time-eaters as chatty housemates, a super-friendly neighbor, or the lure of household duties.

Drawing on a host of suggestions gleaned from seasoned telecommuters as well as personal experience, I've included sections on how to organize for your days out of the office and how to stay on track at home. In addition, this chapter covers using technology to help keep in focus. Finally, I've provided advice for hotelers and others who share a desk back at the office.

ORGANIZING FOR YOUR DAYS OUT OF THE OFFICE

Successful telecommuting requires planning and forethought. There's nothing more irritating than realizing you've left an important file at the office that you need at home. And, although you may be able to telephone someone and get him or her to look up the information, or fax you a few pages, such requests get old fast. So it's best to get yourself organized.

Identify what you can do from home

Tasks that are most appropriate for telecommuting are those jobs you can do best while working alone. Among them are:

- Drafting a report
- Preparing a proposal
- Analyzing data
- Conducting research
- Scheduling appointments
- Using online resources
- Conducting telephone interviews
- Reading and responding to e-mail
- Developing a budget

Go through your calendar from the last few weeks and note what tasks and activities you performed. Mark any that you could have accomplished at a site other than your main office. Make a note of the kinds of equipment and materials you used.

Once you've made your list, decide which tasks you could effectively do from home (or at another location). Reexamine the number of meetings you attended. Could some of them be handled just as effectively (and in less time) via a teleconference?

Could you rearrange your schedule to allow more time for solo tasks? For example, by grouping your meetings, you may be able to free up a day or two for off-site work.

Determine what you need where

For a few days before you begin to telecommute, keep a running list of the files, references, and equipment you've used. Tally the frequency as well. Don't forget to note software accessed.

Then analyze your list. Decide what papers you use often and determine whether you can duplicate them for use in both offices. In some cases, it makes sense to make a copy for each location. In others, it's more logical to plan to work on a project with multiple, hard-copy references in the office and do less research-heavy tasks at home. If at all possible, try to get the files you need on disk. It's much easier to tote changes and updates as computer files, rather than as paper.

Consider a dry run: Get your office-mates to communicate with you as if you already were at home by phone, fax, or e-mail. No dropping by your office or posting a note on your partition. AT&T's financial network services group conducted just such a telecommuting rehearsal. According to manager Bob Kopp, "We set aside a week where we pretended that we were already at home. It really worked out a lot of bugs right there."

If you plan ahead carefully, you'll be able to reduce what you tote to reasonable dimensions. Some useful tips:

- Arrange with your company to get legal copies of software you'll use at both home and office.

- Don't forget to take home a copy of the company telephone list. It's easy to overlook and you'll be lost without it.

- Be sure you know how to use the software you need before you strike out on your own. Ditto with the technology.

- Remember to update your voice mail. You'll want to provide status to callers and change it daily. For example:

> **You've reached the desk of George Washington. Today is Tuesday, January 24th, and I'll be working from home today and tomorrow. If your call is urgent, call my home office at 202-555-5555; otherwise, leave a message and I'll return your call when I'm back in the office.**

- If you don't want to provide your home office number over voice mail or answering machine, arrange for a paging service to contact you when a message awaits.

Avoid lugging stuff back and forth

You can often spot a neophyte telecommuter by the amount of stuff he or she carries to and from the office. Many end up carrying two or more bagfuls in each direction, something consultant Jack Nilles calls "The Two-Briefcase Syndrome." Save your back by planning ahead.

USE REMOTE ACCESS TO STAY IN CONTROL

Using remote access software, you can dial up your company's mainframe or your personal computer at work and operate it as though it was sitting right in front of you. This makes it easy to run programs on your remote machine without having to have the program on your hard drive. You can also keep your laptop and desktop synchronized.

Avoid the two-briefcase syndrome

With remote access software, you can update files, check your e-mail, print reports, synchronize files, and use office-based applications as though you were in the office. Eric Fecci, a managing partner with Posner & Fecci, a CPA firm in White Plains, New York, uses pcAnywhere from Symantec (*www.symantec.com*) to stay in touch with accounting clients. The program allows Fecci to access information from a client's network, thus avoiding the drive to a client site. The software especially came in handy when Fecci broke his leg, effectively grounding him for months. Working from home, he was able to complete all his work, with no change in customer service.

The software can perform a variety of tasks for you. For example, pcAnywhere has a callback feature that allows you to dial the host computer at the office, log on, and promptly hang up. The system immediately calls the home computer back. This security feature prevents others from accessing the system. It can also save you money on long-distance charges. Other handy features include password protection, file encryption, and automatic file synchronization. See *Resources*, at the end of this chapter, for other remote-control software vendors.

Remote power switch control

If you have no office LAN and want to access your computer at work, you either have to leave it on (and pray that some frugal soul doesn't turn it off) or get a power control device such as Dataprobe's PowerPal (*www.dataprobe.com*) or Deltronix' Remote Power Switch (*www.deltronix.com*). These devices sit between the office modem and the electrical outlet. You program the number of rings that will wake up your computer. Then, to turn it on, call, wait until you've reached your ring threshold, and enter an activation code. Your computer stays on during your remote session and then turns itself off after the call is terminated.

STAYING ORGANIZED AT HOME

I've assembled some tips from telecommuting pros that may help you stay focused.

■ **Set goals**

Set specific goals for what you expect to accomplish on your days at home. Review them at the beginning and end of each day. Stick to your deadlines. If you did not meet an expected deadline, determine why.

■ **Stay connected**

If you're going to be working at another site, or will be mobile on a particular day, arrange for a way for your office to reach you. This could be via a pager or cellular phone. Alternatively, you might be able to leave the telephone number of the office you're working in for the day. Just be sure that the receptionist at the temporary work site knows who you are—and how to reach you.

■ **Stick to a schedule**

Wake at a reasonable hour, have breakfast, get dressed, and get to your office. Don't dawdle, read the entire newspaper, or do household chores.

■ **Set up rituals that help you start and stop work**

Telecommuters often need signals or rituals that help them start and end their workday. My day begins when I head down the hall with my coffee, fire up my Mac, and download my e-mail. Matt Halpin, an accountant in Durham, North Carolina, actually walks out his front door, around the house, and into the back door, even though he could easily reach his office through the den. At the end of the day, he reverses the process.

■ **Stay in touch with the office**

Keep your manager and team members informed of your progress. Be sure to be available for their calls. Don't let a day go by without communicating with the office at least twice. This could take the form of voice and e-mail too, but it's preferable to have at least one real-time voice conversation daily.

DEALING WITH DISTRACTIONS

When you were working in the office, you probably had at least one work-wrecking pest, who roamed the aisles, looking for someone to shoot the bull with. Stopping by to talk about last night's TV action or tomorrow's game can be enjoyable—within limits. You learned how to set those limits at work, but now you have to cope with a whole new set of distractions from your children, other family members, pets, neighbors, even telemarketers and deliverymen.

Kids

Don't for a minute consider combining telecommuting with caring for your children. You can't. It's impossible to divide your attention between your children and your work. Both will suffer.

You'll need to work out child-care arrangements. If you've got the room, and the ability to concentrate, have a babysitter or nanny on-site. That way, you can take breaks or lunch with your child. The downside of this arrangement is that it can be difficult to get back to work.

Once your children are school-age, you may be able to have them in the home while you work. Though it's pleasurable to have your children with you, you need to set strict guidelines to keep children and work separate. Otherwise, your little ones may interrupt your work or alienate your callers.

Anna Quindlen, when still working as a columnist at the *New York Times*, often worked at home to spend more time with her three children and to get some uninterrupted think time in. She reported, in an article in *Working Woman* ("Why I Quit," December 1995) that things could sometimes get pretty crazy. One day her son Christopher casually told her that "some man just called but I told him you couldn't talk because you were making dinner." Quindlen learned the next day that the caller was Jesse Jackson, who wanted to update her about the current situation in Haiti.

You'll need to set up some work rules for your children, or you'll go nuts. Here are mine:

■ Don't use Mom's work computer.

■ If I'm on the phone, write me a note.

■ My office has a door for a reason. If it is closed, just pop your head in to let me know you're home and then close the door again.

■ Don't borrow my office equipment. If you do, put it back. This has worked only partially successfully in my home—my scissors migrate to the kitchen several times a week and my stapler has a habit of visiting the den.

■ Never answer the business line.

■ If somehow you do answer my telephone anyway, be professional when you take the message. Don't provide the caller with any details. That means do not say that your mom is in the bathroom or taking a nap or out weeding or anything at all.

A final note: *School vacations can be very trying. You may want to investigate day camp or other supervised activities to take your child out of the home.*

Elders

Many people successfully combine telecommuting with eldercare. If your live-in parent is bedridden, you'll need in-home help. If your parent is mobile but doesn't drive, you might look into an adult day activity program. Otherwise, you can use the same rules you use for your children. Good luck enforcing them, however.

Pets

I love working with my pets around. They're great company and, for the most part, are satisfied to nap or watch me work. I do draw the line, however, when I'm on the phone. Frisby, one of my cats, has learned how to hang up the phone. He sits on top of my monitor and waits until I'm not looking. Then he hurls himself at the phone, hitting the flash button. Charming.

Dogs can be a challenge, too. If you have one that barks at helicopters, delivery people, and just about anything else that moves, you might need to work on silence training. If that's not successful, there's always the option of shutting the door.

Neighbors and visitors

I found it tough at first to convince my friends and neighbors that I was working at home and was *not* available to pick up their kids from school, take in their deliveries, babysit their sick child, take a two-hour coffee break, participate in their favorite charity, hang out, drive them to the airport, pick up their laundry—you name it.

Get ready for an onslaught of requests and have your answers prepared. Practice many ways of saying no. If necessary, invoke your boss's name. "No, I can't take little Johnny to soccer practice for you, my boss would . . " Cite deadlines (even if you don't have any that day). "I can't drive your mom to the mall. My budget report has to be in by 6 p.m." Mention dire consequences. "I'd like to have lunch with you today but, if I don't get this report done, they may yank me back into the office." Lie. "I can't get away right now. I'm expecting an important phone call."

Household chores

Not all telecommuters suffer from householditis, but if you find yourself hunting down stray cobwebs when you should be studying budgets or sneaking in a quick pass of the vacuum when you really need to proofread your presentation, you've got a problem. You must train yourself to ignore household chores during your normal work hours.

On the other hand, it's okay to perform the occasional simple household task during a mini-break while brewing a cup of coffee. Telecommuters need breaks, just like their in-office brethren. If you want to spend your breaktime with a dust mop, and can perform the chore in five minutes or less, go ahead and dust away.

COMMUNICATING WITH THE OFFICE

It's easy to stay visible and in control if you remember to keep communication as your most important goal.

- If you're new to telecommuting, you may find that your colleagues are reluctant to call you at home. They may feel uncomfortable or may think that they're bothering you when they call. This newfound politeness needs to be nipped in the bud! You need to stay in contact with your coworkers now, more than ever. If no one is calling you, call them.

- Let your office know your work hours at home and be sure to make yourself available to answer the phone. If, for some reason, you have to leave your home office, inform someone at your office. And leave an informative message on your voice mail or answering machine. Whatever you do, don't leave without letting someone know where you're going and when you'll be back.

- On the days you're telecommuting, be sure to answer your home office phone in a professional manner. If you just pick up the phone and say "Hello," you'll confuse your business callers. If you're unsure what to say, a simple "Good morning" or "Good afternoon," followed by your name, will be fine.

- What can you do if someone from your office calls you *after* your normal working hours? If such calls are infrequent, it's not really such a problem. However, if people in your office begin to behave as though you're on call 12 hours a day, you'll need to put your foot down. Gently explain that you'll take care of the problem tomorrow and ask that they call within your established office hours in the future.

- When you find that you need to leave the home office during the day, group errands efficiently. Try to keep outside tasks to a minimum. Be sure to let your office know that you'll be unavailable, and estimate when you'll return.

TIPS FOR STAYING VISIBLE

Many telecommuters fear that they'll be overlooked for promotions and other perks, once they're out of sight. Though studies show that telecommuters actually get promoted more often than their in-office counterparts, the fear remains. The best way to conquer fear is to take charge, so here are some suggestions for staying visible.

Dennell Dickey, who telecommutes full time, felt uncomfortable just working on project goals and keeping her manager informed on an occasional basis. Because she's very results-oriented, and her projects have long lead times, she sends a weekly status report to her boss using the following headings:

■ **This week's accomplishments**

Shows weekly results. Helps keep her on target.

■ **Next week's activities**

Helps plan out the next week.

■ **Let's talk about**

Opens a dialog on concerns that don't fit the other categories.

■ **For your information**

A method for communicating problems, vacation plans, doctor's appointments, and so on.

According to Dickey, her system works great. "I have the opportunity to show results weekly. And, if next week's activities aren't on target, my boss can give me that feedback."

DEALING WITH ISOLATION

Many telecommuters sorely miss their daily dose of social interaction. And, if you're accustomed to working closely with a team, you may also miss the opportunity to be with colleagues, and the synergy that can come from such dialogue. If you're just telecommuting a day or two a week, you can probably get along okay with less office socializing. But, if you telecommute more frequently, you'll have to deal with the isolation and come to terms with it.

First, recognize that you need people. If you can't see them, arrange to interact with them frequently in other ways. Send lots of e-mail. Call in to chat and check up on work status. Find out what's going on in the office grapevine.

Many telecommuters arrange to have lunch outside their office every day, just so they can interact with people. Tanja Wilson, a programmer/analyst who telecommutes full time from her home in Noblesville, Indiana, doesn't always remember to make time for lunch but comments that, "If I were in the office, and I remembered to take lunch, I would actually be OUT and unavailable. My office can't expect me to always be available 24 hours a day. After all, telecommuting is not house arrest." Roy McKenzie telecommutes three days a week from his home in San Francisco. McKenzie takes a daily break at a local coffeehouse. There, he joins a regular group of telecommuters and solo entrepreneurs for a short and lively chat session.

Don't overlook the usefulness of online support. Many telecommuters take a break in forums such as CompuServe's Working From Home forum, (*http://go.compuserve.com/WorkFromHome*), chat rooms such as the Mining Company's telecommute section (*www.telecommuting.miningco.com*), or message boards such as Parent Soup's telecommuting area (*www.parentsoup.com*).

All your interaction need not be work-related, either. A portion of the time spent at the office is just pure socializing—bragging about a new grandchild, chatting about what to serve for a holiday meal, shooting the bull about your favorite team. You need to set up a method that works for you. A novel approach is used by Bill Holtz, vice president of global enterprise services at Nortel. Holtz, a full-time telecommuter, conferences with his worldwide staff through e-mail and a videoconference link installed in his basement. Shortly after his daughter was born, he introduced her to his staff over the televised link. "It was great," he says. "I think that personal interaction is a very important part of team building."

If you're starting to feel depressed or sluggish, you'll probably perk up by relocating your work station near a window. Studies at the University of Michigan have shown that people who work under natural light report fewer illnesses, sharper concentration, and increased productivity. Hey, it's your office—who says you can't have a window in it?

I vary my routine by taking my proofreading and offline research duties to the back patio (if it's warm and sunny) or the breakfast table (if it's not). I carry a portable phone to be instantly available to callers.

ARE YOU A WORKAHOLIC?

If you're just starting out as a telecommuter, you'll naturally strive to optimize your performance level. After all, you want to ensure that your boss and coworkers are happy with the situation so that you can continue to telecommute. But there comes a time when you should begin to reap the rewards of telecommuting—and that means slowing down and taking time to smell the roses.

Some telecommuters have trouble stopping work when they're at home. "My work is always there waiting for me," says Maryanne Kroeber, a virtual office worker in San Antonio, Texas. "I'd pass by my office and see that pile of stuff on my desk. I'd tell myself it'll just take me a minute to clean it up. Three hours later, I'd look up and realize my evening was completely gone."

When the office is in your home, the office can take over. You need to make a psychological division between work and home. One way to do this is to establish an end-of-work routine—take your daughter to the park or follow the office pattern and clean off your desktop, make a to-do list for the next day, and do a final e-mail check. Attorney Shelly Greenberg, a reformed workaholic, closes and *locks* the door to her home office.

Be sure to take regular breaks. It's easy to forget them when you're working alone. There's no one dropping by your office to suggest that you get a cup of coffee together. When you remember to take a break, your efficiency will probably go up, because you'll return to work refreshed.

Breaks don't have to be long to make a difference. Consider taking a mini-break. Do something entirely nonwork-related. I dash outside and weed for 10 minutes or give my cats a thorough brushing. Kevin Morrison, a Chicago-based designer, takes his dog for a walk every lunchtime. Great for the dog, great for Kevin.

Contrary to what you may have learned at school, fidgeting is good for you. Sitting is hard on your back. In fact, researchers at Haworth, an office furniture company, learned that sitting for too long causes mental drowsiness and fatigue, which impacts performance and productivity. So don't sit up straight, or stay in any position for too long. Get up, move around, and walk somewhere at least once every hour.

Steps for avoiding becoming a workaholic

Alice Bredin writes the syndicated column, Working at Home, and is author of *The Home Office Solution*. She suggests the following ideas for avoiding overwork:

- Learn to differentiate between what is truly urgent and what is not. If it's not urgent, maybe it can wait.

- Don't try to prove anything. You will probably automatically be more productive when you work outside of the office. Don't work extra hard to prove you can do it. You're not carrying the future of telecommuting on your shoulders.

- Designate time when you're not available. These are mental breaktimes when you unplug your phone and turn off your beeper. If people call you on the weekends or after hours, offer to call them back during office hours or wrap up quickly, making it obvious you do not want to talk on the phone.

- Don't use all your commute time for work. Take advantage of the time gained to improve the quality of your life. Do something fun!

- Acknowledge your accomplishments. At the end of the day go over the tasks you have completed—even small ones such as phone calls or filing. This may keep you from punishing yourself because you feel you never get anything done.

PROHIBIT PROCRASTINATION

If you're like me, tomorrow is often the busiest day of the week in my schedule. If procrastination is a worry, try these time-tested anti-postponement techniques:

■ Do what you hate the most first thing in the morning

I'm not sure why this one works so well, but take it from me, it works every time. You end up feeling so good the hateful task is out of the way that it energizes the rest of your day.

■ Break tasks up into small, manageable chunks

A large task doesn't look as daunting when seen in its parts. The additional planning involved in taking this step helps you plan the task better.

■ Avoid time-wasting behaviors

Schedule your day and limit the amount of time you set aside for jobs that tend to take too long. For example, if you find yourself spending excessive time reading and responding to e-mail, tightly schedule the time you allot to it.

■ Develop back-to-work cues

Should you find yourself taking frequent breaks at home, or staying on break far too long, try setting a timer when you get up from your desk. When it chimes, it's back to the grind.

Set up regular work hours and stick to them. Deviate only when you have an emergency project to complete.

USE TECHNOLOGY TO KEEP ON FOCUS

Thankfully, technology has taken some of the stress out of getting organized. There are all sorts of programs designed for the forgetful, disorganized, or overscheduled worker.

There's a wide variety of PIM (Personal Information Manager) software designed to help you keep a grip on the many facets of your life—appointments, address books, dates, names, phone numbers, birthdays, fax numbers, and even memos. The best PIMs let you create several address books so you can organize information by project, take notes, handle to-do lists, create calendars, and reconcile differences between the PIM files on your desktop and notebook computers. A nice feature is the ability to dial from the desktop, just by highlighting the number desired. You need a modem to do this, but it sure saves time (and wrong numbers).

More sophisticated PIMs are often called contact managers. My contact manager, Symantec's ACT!, lets me create form letters, schedule follow-up calls, and even print my calendar and address book for handy reference. Using a special software interface, I can download ACT files to my Palm Pilot and easily take my calendar and contacts on the road. PIMs are great. To help you find one, I've listed a bunch of popular programs in *Resources*, at the end of this chapter.

If you need to keep close track of your hours in order to report back to the home office, consider getting a copy of Symantec's pcTelecommute (*www.symantec.com*). One of its features, Work Monitor, creates an activity log that you can submit to your manager. The program tracks your workday, and lists the files you created, modified, or accessed, as well as calls made and received. In addition to the work monitoring features, pcTelecommute contains handy tools for remote access and control, faxing, virus protection, and call screening.

Pete Durst, a computer instructor based in Ottawa, Canada, uses pcTelecommute to retrieve work from his office, work on it at home, and get it back to the office easily. "Using pcTelecommute has been a big time-saver," he says. By using a feature called DayEnd Sync, he was able to easily synchronize changed files at the end of each workday.

MEANWHILE, BACK AT THE OFFICE

You'll want to maximize your efficiency on your days in the office as well. Points to remember:

■ Plan ahead

Plan your office time for face-to-face meetings, team sessions, use of office equipment, and the like.

■ Set up a telecommuter bulletin board

Post a calendar in a convenient spot that shows what days you will be telecommuting and the numbers where you may be reached.

■ Be kind to office support staff

Their opportunities for telecommuting are limited, yet their help makes it possible for you to telecommute easily. Be lavish with praise and thank yous. Trade favors. Give gifts.

■ Don't stint on office sociability

If you've been left off the list for contributing to the office football pool, holiday party, or retirement gathering, speak up. You don't want to be thought of as a Scrooge or a hermit. Those social events cement working relationships and are important.

SHARING A DESK

Many telecommuters share a desk back at the office. It works something like this: Sam gets the office on Monday through Wednesday and Sara has it Thursday and Friday. This arrangement sounds great—on paper. But it's up to the two of them to make it work in reality.

Sharing an office raises all sorts of territorial issues. You'll need to work out arrangements for:

- Who gets what drawers in the desk and file cabinet
- How to share directories and files on the office computer
- How customizable software should be set up
- How to handle voice and paper mail
- What to do if you run out of storage space
- Where to put desktop items such as pencil holders and in-out bins

- What to do on the rare occasions when both of you need to be in the office
- What to put on the walls

The office support staff can get pretty mixed up about office ownership, too. Some companies put both names on the cubicle outside; others use velcro-backed identifiers. Whoever is in sticks his or her name on the door.

If your office runs on the hotel principle, you won't have a permanent desk of your own. You'll just check in, find out what cubicle you're assigned to, and camp out there for the day. If you miss seeing your family photos or kid pix, carry one or two on disk, as *gif* or *jpeg* files, and display them on your virtual desktop.

RESOURCES

Books

The Virtual Office Survival Handbook: What Telecommuters and Entrepreneurs Need to Succeed in Today's Nontraditional Workplace
by Alice Bredin
John Wiley & Sons, 1996

The Ultimate Home Office Survival Guide
by Sunny & Kim Baker
Peterson's Guides, 1998

Home Office Solutions: How to Balance Your Professional and Personal Lives While Working at Home
by Alice Bredin & Kirsten M. Lagatree
John Wiley & Sons, 1998

PIMs & contact managers

ACT!
Symantec
www.symantec.com

Day-Timer
Day-Timer Technologies
www.daytimer.com

GoldMine
GoldMine Software
www.goldminesw.com

Microsoft Outlook
Microsoft
www.microsoft.com

Lotus Organizer
Lotus Development Corp.
www.lotus.com

Remote access & control software

Carbon Copy
Compaq
www.compaq.com

LapLink
Traveling Software
www.travsoft.com

Timbuktu
Farallon Computing
www.farallon.com

ReachOut
Stac Electronics
www.stac.com

pcAnywhere32
Symantec
www.symantec.com

CHAPTER 9

Working on the Road

PICK UP ANY NEWSPAPER OR MAGAZINE and you'll see ads extolling the virtues of the anywhere, anytime workplace. Hordes of digital cowboys (a.k.a. road warriors) are working from planes, hotel rooms, borrowed offices, boats, cars, even RVs. These stalwarts pack a pager, portable PC, and mobile phone, and set up a temporary worksite wherever and whenever the mood strikes.

Sometimes it's easy to work remotely, sometimes not. Getting and staying connected are the major hurdles. Remote workers must figure out how to connect at a phone booth, restaurant, hard-wired hotel room, or guest office. They must learn how to work with strange phone systems and overcome the perils of digital lines. They struggle to keep their batteries charged, their gear to a minimum, and their costs down. And, if they don't check in with the office on a regular basis, they'll hear about it. A tough challenge.

This chapter discusses several wireless technologies—cellular, pagers, PDAs, and wireless modems. We'll look at equipment designed for the well-equipped road warrior, provide clues about modeming remotely, and learn how to make international connections. I've included loads of tips for working anywhere and staying connected—tips I've discovered myself or learned from other seasoned telecommuters. Finally, I've included a road warrior's survival kit.

Other chapters in the book also contain useful information for working remotely. For information on remote-control software and document conferencing, take a look at chapter 10 (Working Together). Chapter 4 (Coping With E-mail) and chapter 6 (Handling Fax) also have sections dedicated to mobile workers.

PACK A PAGER

You'll need to keep in touch with the office and be able to get e-mail and other messages while on the road. Studies indicate that the chance of a business call reaching you on the first try is less than 20 percent. Having a pager or other wireless communication device increases your odds considerably. In fact, by using a pager, you can reduce callbacks by 90 percent. A pager frees you from waiting by the phone or playing endless rounds of telephone tag.

Pagers are very reliable. They were originally designed for doctors and others requiring emergency communications. Tough, durable, and able to work in a variety of adverse conditions, pagers often run for over a month on a single set of inexpensive batteries. Pagers reach spots other systems can't, such as the interiors of steel office buildings, tunnels, and subways. During natural disasters and other emergencies, when telephone systems may be down, paging is often the only communications network still in operation.

Paging devices come in all flavors—from simple numeric pagers to sophisticated wireless wonders. Some pose as wristwatches; others are camouflaged as fountain pens. Some strap onto your ankle (ideal for bikers and joggers); others hang around your neck or clip onto your belt. Some pagers let you program them to play special tunes, even ones you compose.

Worldwide paging is even possible via PageNet's Iridium World Page Service (*www.pagenet.com*).

Pager choices

Plain old beeper

Think of this as a radio-controlled doorbell. The pager buzzes or beeps to let you (and everyone around you) know that you're being paged. If you dislike the sound, many devices vibrate silently. You call your pager service to pick up the message.

Numeric pager

Displays the phone number you should call. If your paging service is connected to voice mail or a fax mailbox, the number displayed will be the service access number. If your callers directly page you, the number displayed will be the number they keyed in:

> 415-555-4727

Alphanumeric pager

Displays a brief message (which could also include a phone number) or coded information such as a sender code:

> BRING THE HIGGINS FILE WITH YOU TO THE 9AM
> BRIEFING TODAY

Alpha pagers reduce the number of return calls you have to make. Some of them can display short e-mail messages.

Two-way pager

Displays a brief message. Some allow you to answer as you wish; others require that you choose from a short list of preset responses (such as Yes, No, Will Call You Later, or Traffic Delay).

> 10 AM MEETING CANCELED
> WHEN TO RESCHEDULE?
> 1. THIS FRI AT 10AM?
> 2. NEXT TUES AT 3PM?

Voice pager

Motorola makes a 5.5-ounce portable answering machine called the Pocketalk, which uses pager technology. It lets you get your voice mail on the go without having to make a call.

PC message receiver

You can purchase a PC card with paging capability that fits into the Type II PC (or PCMCIA) slot in your laptop or handheld computer. The PC message receiver is especially useful for sending or receiving time-sensitive information such as price updates, stock availability, and market news.

Internet paging

If you have an alpha pager, check with your paging service to find out how to use Internet messaging service. For example, if you have PageNet service, you provide your customers with your PIN number, and they create an e-mail message on their computer. Then they address the e-mail to your *PIN number @pagenet.net* and the message is sent to your pager. Nextel offers a similar service via the Internet (*phone number @nextel.com*).

Warning: *Don't expect Internet paging to be quite as fast as the regular paging network. Use another method when the message is urgent and especially during peak Internet traffic hours.*

Hook your answering machine to a pager

If you have an answering machine in your home office and need to know when it receives a message, you can attach a device that alerts your pager when a message has been received. If you're shopping for a new answering machine, look for one with built-in paging capability.

Are pagers secure?

Not entirely. Now that many pagers have messaging capability, e-mail pagers are being targeted by hackers who change security codes and take over mailboxes. If this is done to you, your security code won't work and you'll be unable to pick up messages. Ask your paging company to change your security code for you. If the information you need to send is highly sensitive, use more secure communications such as landline phones. Also, to reduce the chances of being targeted, change your password often and avoid easy-to-crack passwords.

CARRY A MOBILE PHONE

Not all telecommuters need a mobile phone. However, if you're always on call, or spend a lot of time in your car or at a field site where a landline phone is not readily available, a wireless phone might be just the ticket.

Garry Mathiason, a partner at a major employment law firm based in San Francisco, uses his cellular phone as regularly as his office phone. When driving between appointments, Mathiason uses his office-on-the road, a Lexus with built-in cell phone. The microphone is implanted in the steering wheel for hands-free talking.

Pay attention to charges

Mobile service can be expensive. Your company will pay a one-time setup fee as well as three types of monthly charges: a monthly subscription cost, a fee for landline services (calls for directory assistance, for example), and an air time charge (the actual time you spent using your cellular phone). The first two charges are fixed, but the air time charges can add up alarmingly fast.

Unlike regular telephone service, the mobile subscriber pays for *both* incoming and outgoing calls. In addition to the monthly access charge, you're charged per minute for the time you spend on the system. Some wireless phone companies are considering a new pricing scheme where the caller pays for incoming calls, so be sure to check for "calling party pays" plans.

The best way to control costs is to give out your cellular number to only a select few, or to combine cellular with a numeric paging service. Arrange for your voice mail or paging service to beep your pager and display the number of the caller. You then dial out on your cellular phone.

Consider renting a cell phone when you need one. Some car rental agencies are including them as standard equipment. Alamo, Avis, Budget, and Hertz offer cellular phones on many of their rental models.

Ways to control roaming charges

Mobile phone service, unlike land-based phone service, is location-dependent. You're allowed to make and receive calls within your calling area. If you travel to another city, and want to use your phone, you'll be operating in another calling area and will be *roaming*. Any calls made while out of your calling area will be charged at the rate of the host carrier, and may cost quite a bit more than your home rate. Some roaming charges run as high as $3 a day and 90¢ a minute. Fortunately, the trend is toward eliminating roaming fees.

If you plan to roam a lot, it's a good idea to arrange for more than one NAM (Numeric Assignment Module)—a chip

installed by the dealer that contains your unique cellular phone number. Most cell phones come with room for two NAMs; some allow up to six. If you have multiple NAMs, you can register your car phone with several different cellular providers and avoid roaming charges.

Incidentally, long-distance charges are often charged at daytime rates, regardless of the time you call. To avoid the expense, use your calling card when roaming.

Hush—you're in a cellular-free zone

You may find yourself in a restaurant that posts a notice stating that the area is a "cellular-free zone." What to do? Well, if you can't bear to turn off your phone, consider replacing the battery with VibraRing, a rechargeable battery that vibrates like a pager when you receive an incoming call (Ora Electronics, *www.orausa.com*). Just be sure to wear your phone—don't tuck it into a purse or briefcase.

What about privacy?

Mobile calls aren't always safe from prying ears. Though not as insecure as cordless phone calls, electronic eavesdropping is still possible. Conversations can be overheard by some types of radio receivers and scanners. If your calls are sensitive and must be secure, avoid analog cellular phones. Use a PCS or digital cellular phone —the digital models are much more difficult to tap than analog cellular phones. For the same reason, don't give out your credit card numbers over cell phones.

Warning: Beware of cellular fraud

If you carry an analog cellular phone, be on the lookout for signs of cellular fraud, and especially for lurking phone cloners. Cloners steal the ID and serial numbers programmed into cellular phones by monitoring cellular traffic and literally lifting phone numbers and ID numbers out of the air. They then install the stolen numbers into another cellular phone and sell it. All calls made on the cloned phone are billed to the legitimate customer. Many cloned phones are sold to criminals— drug dealers and smugglers; others go to people attracted by the lure of a "no-bill" phone. You may not know that your number has been cloned until you receive a huge phone bill.

How can you spot the signs of cloning? It's tricky. If you experience frequent interrupted or dropped calls, you may be "bumping into" the person using your cloned number attempting to make or receive a call at the same time as you. Because both calls are trying to use the same cellular channel, the calls "collide" and the later call knocks the earlier one off the air. Don't just assume that these dropped calls are caused by bad equipment or an overloaded system.

Tips for safeguarding your cell phone:

- If you experience interrupted or terminated calls, frequent wrong numbers, and hangups, report them to your cellular company immediately.

- Don't permit access to your car phone to service people you don't know. When you use a valet service or get your car washed, take your phone with you or lock it in the trunk.

- Avoid using your phone in or near airports, business centers, and other areas with high cellular use.

- Review your monthly bills carefully and report discrepancies immediately.

- Don't allow your cellular number to be published on company phone lists. Don't print it on your business cards. Write it in if someone needs it.

Send a fax via cellular

Yes, you can send or receive a fax over your cellular phone service. One way to fax remotely is to plug your fax modem into the RJ-11 phone jack of your cellular phone and dial the desired fax number. Or get a phone with fax and modem capabilities built in. Another option is to buy a PC cellular fax modem; the device connects into a cellular or landline phone using a built-in interface and lets you send and receive faxes into your computer from virtually anywhere.

Warning: *Stop driving when you're using cellular fax in a mobile phone. You need a strong, clear signal to maintain a fax transmission.*

Keep costs in mind. Every minute that you are connected over a cellular service costs from 20¢ to 99¢, depending on service package, time of day, and where you are located. Thus, a three-minute local call to send a fax will cost between 60¢ and $2.97.

Get e-mail over your phone

Some digital wireless phone companies offer e-mail service. For example, AT&T's PocketNet service gives you wireless phone service as well as unlimited e-mailing and an online address book (*www.pocketnet.com*). Another possibility is the Nokia 9000il Communicator. This flexible device is a GSM digital phone, two-way pager, web browser, e-mail manager, and fax machine (*www.nokia.com*).

WIRELESS DATA

If you want to send and receive e-mail or hitch up to the Internet, but don't have a phone connection, there are several technologies that will let you connect. If you need a wireless way to get your e-mail, check out one of these options:

ARDIS

Advanced Radio Data Information Services (800-662-5328) is a packet-switched data network service that provides e-mail, wireless fax, and operator-assisted messaging.

CDPD

Cellular Digital Packet Data offers faster connections (up to 19.2 Kbps). This technology sends packets of data over the analog cellular network. CDPD is available through your local cellular carriers and works with a wireless PC Card, complete with a tiny antenna.

Cellular data

This works with your normal cellular service and a cell phone equipped with a modem interface. Like cellular fax, analog cellular data transmission is error-prone and costly. A 10-minute call to send and receive e-mail will cost between $2 and $8.50.

RAM Mobile Data

This service relies on transmitting stations to send and receive data. This service is limited to text-based data, such as e-mail and fax.

Ricochet

The Ricochet Wireless Network from Metricom is the most affordable wireless service available. You pay a flat rate for unlimited access, and can use the service for Internet browsing, as well as e-mail access and other standard data services.

MODEMING ON THE ROAD

As I've mentioned previously, using your modem on unfamiliar phone lines carries a risk. If you suddenly find that your modem is not working when you plug it into an unfamiliar jack, you may be in for some very bad news. Many hotels, universities, and larger office buildings have digital lines. Most modems can't take the higher electrical current that runs over the phone lines of digital phone systems.

If your modem encounters those lines, it will die on the spot. Seasoned travelers carry a testing device to test the telephone port before attaching a modem. IBM makes one that's easy to use—you just insert the test plug in the phone jack. If the line is analog and safe to use, you see a green light. You could also purchase a modem with a built-in line tester such as the 3Com Megahertz 56K Global Modem PC Card. This credit-card sized modem alerts you if connecting to potentially damaging digital or PBX phone lines. If you find your modem is in danger, you have several options: don't use it, call from a pay phone with a modular plug, use a service bureau, or employ a special connector that eliminates the incompatibility.

Once you've determined that the line is digital, you'll need a device that converts the digital signal to analog in order for your modem to work. The best source of converters is TeleAdapt (*www.teleadapt.com*).

EQUIPMENT FOR THE ROAD WARRIOR

Remote workers carry a variety of equipment on the road, ranging from a simple pager to the elaborate accoutrements of a full-fledged office. Here are some of their favorite out-of-office accessories:

Pack a portable

Most often listed as "the single piece of equipment I couldn't live without," a portable computer is often essential. The lighter the better. Look for one that has a built-in pointing device (one less thing to carry; easier to use on a crowded plane). You'll also want a built-in modem or a Group II PC slot for a modem card.

Discover docking

A docking station might be a good move for those of you who carry a portable to and from the office. Docks make it easier to connect at either end—you just couple the laptop to the dock, using a special docking connector. This lets you use a larger monitor, a full-size keyboard, or the multimedia capabilities on your desktop without having to replicate them for the road.

Not all docking stations are controlled by a single connector—some require that you plug in every device. This could require disconnecting and reconnecting several plugs. In addition, you may have to change your system and video configuration every time you dock. To avoid that hassle, ask your tech support to help you set up multiple configuration files that you can easily switch between.

Docking stations are often proprietary so be sure to check with your vendor before dashing out to get one. CNF sells a universal port replicator, dubbed the Bus (*www.cnfinc.com*). The

Bus plugs into the PC Card slot on almost any notebook. You connect all your peripherals into the Bus, and you're ready to roll.

Divide your files

It's a good idea to carry important files separately from your laptop. That way, if you lose your laptop (or it gets stolen), company secrets are secure. A couple of ways to accomplish this: Use a removable hard drive or a cartridge drive such as Iomega's Zip Drive (*www.iomega.com*) or a type III PC card hard disk drive.

Many portables have smaller hard drives than the ones you're used to in the office. Should you find yourself needing to save a megafile and don't have sufficient space left on your hard drive, try this trick: send yourself an e-mail and attach the chubby file to the message. Then, when you're back in the office, download the file to your desktop computer.

Scan it in

Hate carrying around paper? Scan the document into your computer and leave the paper behind. Visioneer (*www.visioneer.com*) makes the PaperPort, a portable scanner that is about the size of a box of plastic wrap and weighs in at 2½ pounds. Visioneer makes versions for both Macs and PCs.

Check your calling card

Your long-distance carrier may be levying a surcharge for each calling-card call you make. These range from 50¢ to 90¢ a call. Shop around for a long-distance company that charges no fee. Often, your best deal will come from a long-distance reseller. Many of them offer no-surcharge calling cards.

Get a personal toll-free number

If you make a lot of calls back to the home office, get a personal toll-free number. Sometimes you can get one free if you purchase other services. Usage fees range around 20¢ to 25¢ per minute.

Forward your faxes

Arrange for a fax mailbox if you need access to your faxes on the road. JFAX (*www.jfax.com*) and SkyTel (*www.skytel.com*) offer this service.

Acquire a follow-me number

If you travel frequently, consider signing up for a follow-me-anywhere number. That way, your calls are automatically forwarded to the number (or numbers) you specify.

Sign up for a secretary

Need a receptionist to field your calls and messages? Consider signing up for Wildfire (*www.wildfire.com*), an automated secretarial service. Wildfire can return calls to people who leave messages, keep track of your whereabouts, even interrupt a call and whisper the name of an incoming caller. You can then decide whether to take the call or send it to voice mail. When you call your Wildfire service, you're greeted with a summary of your messages. You can pick which messages to hear now and which to save for later. If you need to call someone back, you just command Wildfire to dial for you. Wildfire already has the number stored in memory. Service fees can be somewhat hefty. An average user can rack up charges of $150 to $200 a month.

Use software to stay in sync

Symantec's pcTelecommute (*www.symantec.com*) offers a whole toolbox of programs for staying in touch with the office. There's an incoming fax mailbox, a caller ID function that logs incoming calls, a work log that keeps track of all files you worked on, remote access software for contacting your office LAN, and even an automatic synchronization program that matches your home PC with your office PC and uploads changed files.

Leave your laptop

Are you sure you need to lug that six-pound portable computer everywhere you go? If all you need is to access your e-mail, there are loads of easier solutions. Take along a handheld device such as Palm Pilot, an alpha pager, or a pocket e-mail device. Or you might try out PocketMail (*www.pocketscience.com*), a device equipped with a tiny screen, a small rubberized keyboard, and a snap-out acoustical modem built into the back. To get your mail, you dial the 800 number, attach the modem cups to the telephone, and your e-mail is downloaded over the phone. Of course, you have to pay a monthly subscription fee of about $10, but it sure beats carrying a heavy notebook, power cord, and modem around.

TIPS FOR WORKING ANYWHERE
At the airport

Should you be worried about sending your laptop, modem, or cell phone through the X-ray machines used for security at airports? No, say most experts. The X-ray itself is harmless to such magnetic media as your hard drive or floppies. However, the electric motor that drives the conveyor belt develops a magnetic field that can harm your data. Most machines in the U.S. shield the motors on conveyors. So you needn't worry about domestic travel. However, if you travel to countries using unshielded 220-volt motors, ask the inspector to allow the equipment to bypass electronic inspection. Be prepared to open everything up and power it on to prove that you're not a terrorist toting an explosive device.

Remember to register your nonAmerican-made electronic equipment with Customs before you leave the U.S. And carry those papers with you to prove where and when you purchased it. Otherwise, you may have to pay a hefty duty when you return.

In the air

It's almost impossible to use your cellular phone in the air because of FCC regulations. And, although the FCC allows cell phone use while a plane is on terra firma, FAA regulations allow airlines to ban cellular use on the ground. Most of them do. If you need to make an in-flight call, use the airline's phones.

Some airlines offer phone service that gives you a personal phone number for the length of your flight. This gives you the ability to *receive* incoming phone calls as well as make outgoing ones. To receive calls, you activate an on-board telephone located in the back of the seat in front of you. By dialing a few digits, you'll be given a special *aircall* number. Then you call your office and give them your special number. Calls are expensive: the minimum charge for a domestic call is about $7; double that for the shortest international chat. One traveler was shocked to get a bill for $1,208 for a 123-minute transatlantic phone call. Far more than the cost of the ticket!

Don't boot up your computer or turn on your portable fax machine until the plane reaches at least 10,000 feet. This is to ensure that the electronic emanations from your equipment don't interfere with cockpit controls.

In your car

Nowadays you can purchase a car with a built-in phone, fax machine, scanner, and GPS (global positioning system). Add a laptop on the seat beside you, and you're ready to go.

Car batteries are terrific power sources. A good way to get double duty out of yours is to plug in an extension cord that allows you to plug two devices into one cigarette lighter. Look for one at your local auto supply store.

If you're going to be traveling by car, carry a cigarette lighter converter—it plugs straight into your computer, connects it to your car battery, and replaces the normal power supply. Another advantage is that you can recharge your computer battery while driving.

The automobile cigarette lighter is standard worldwide. Both the plug and the voltage are reliably the same everywhere. Should you be renting a car abroad, be sure to buy an adapter that works with your particular equipment before you leave home. They're not interchangeable and can be hard to find.

At your hotel

Look for hotels that serve business clients. For example, Marriott now equips some rooms with two power outlets, a

fully adjustable ergonomic chair, a PC modem jack, a mobile writing desk, and a task light. Others provide fax machines, two-line telephones and in-room data ports.

It's also a good idea to book at a hotel that doesn't charge call-access fees if you tend to make lots of long-distance calls. You can search a database of worker-friendly hotels on the Forbes Web site (*www.forbes.com*). Look for "Rooms with a Clue."

When traveling abroad, you'll want to be sure that your hotel has protected phone lines. That's advice from Mike Irwin, who travels frequently in his role as CFO of a major toy company. Irwin learned the hard way that his hotel was not prepared when a power surge traveled up the phone lines and knocked his modem dead.

Use your telephone calling card when making long-distance calls from your hotel. If you don't, you'll end up paying about 40 percent more for each long-distance call. Hotels often charge a fee for using your phone card instead of their phone service. These fees, called access fees, range anywhere from 50¢ to $1.25 a call.

Save money on hotel long-distance by hitting the pound sign between each call instead of hanging up. This will give you a new dial tone and save you from having to reenter your calling card number. More importantly, you'll avoid paying separate calling card access fees.

A telephone debit card might help you save on hotel long-distance charges. These prepaid cards allow you to make nationwide calls at a flat rate. You can buy them in denominations of $10, $25, and so on. To use a debit card, you call the 800 number listed on the card, enter your special PIN code, and dial.

In your RV

Recreational vehicle manufacturers and van conversion companies are developing vehicles especially equipped for the work-on-the-road crowd. You can order a custom mobile office—complete with built-in office furniture, cell phone, printer, modem ports—the works. Starting at $28,000, these offices-on-the-go aren't for everyone, but, if you need a temporary office with bathroom and kitchen conveniences built in, it might make sense.

If you plan to do some serious work from your RV, you might want to check out the North American Roads Travel Network. This organization maintains a searchable list of modem-friendly campgrounds in the U.S. (*www.tl.com*). Another useful resource is Workers on Wheels, a newsletter and online resource for working RVers (*www.workersonwheels.com*).

One tip I learned from truckers: Do your modeming from a truck stop that advertises tabletop phones. It's much easier than trying to get a connection through a phone booth. Ever try to attach couplers and balance your laptop on top of that tiny ledge built into the phone booth that doubles as an elbow rest? Not fun.

On a boat

Can you use a mobile phone on a boat or a cruise? Depends on where you're going. If it's in the Caribbean, contact BoatPhone (800-262-8366; *www.boatphone.com*) which, for around $3 a day, will assign you a local 809 phone number. Calls can be expensive, ranging from $1.75 to $4.50 a minute.

If you're just cruising the inland waterways in your service area, you can use your handheld phone most of the time. However, if you get far from land, your portable won't have the broadcast power to send your signal to the next cell. You'll need a full-powered installed mobile phone if you range far at sea. If you do decide to install a phone on a boat, be sure to get a special marine-quality antenna. Otherwise, it will corrode quickly in the salt air.

For distant cruises, you can arrange for mobile satellite phone service. Contact Comsat (800-424-9152; *www.comsat. com*) or Inmarsat (*www.inmarsat.org*).

On the beach?

Forget those sexy ads showing buffed bodies slaving over their tans while working on their laptops. Unless you adore sand jamming your mouse, suntan lotion gumming up your keyboard, and salt spray misting up your monitor, leave the laptop in the hotel. What's a vacation for, anyway? Enjoy yourself!

If you insist on outdoor computing, be sure to stay in the shade. Excessive heat buildup can severely damage the delicate electronics in your equipment.

Another option is to buy a "ruggedized computer" with watertight door, membrane-covered keyboard, shock mounts, and other devices to protect the computer from various assaults. Some manufacturers of ruggedized units are WPI Husky Computers (*www.husky.co.uk*), Argonaut Computer (*www.argonautcomputer.com*) and Fieldworks (*www.fieldworks. com*).

MAKING INTERNATIONAL CONNECTIONS

The global village is a nice concept—but we're not there yet. Foreign electrical systems and nonstandard phone connections can defeat even the most seasoned traveler. But you can overcome most problems by planning ahead.

If you're used to the reasonable prices of telephone calls in the United States, get ready for a surprise abroad. Hotels in Russia will charge you up to $12 a minute to phone home. A fax from Manila will cost you $10 a page. If the high cost of international long-distance gets to you, try a callback service. Since it costs less to call from the U.S. than from an international hotel, you can save money if your call goes through a U.S. service provider. To use such a service, you dial a callback number from your hotel room, tell the operator your room number and phone number and hang up. A few moments later, you'll get a callback. When you pick up the phone, you're provided with a U.S. dial tone at U.S. rates. If you want to make a number of calls, just press the # (pound) button between calls, instead of hanging up. Where to find such deals? I've listed a few international callback firms in *Resources*, at the end of this chapter.

If you're traveling internationally, arrange for an international access calling card such as AT&T's Corporate Calling Card, MCIWorldCom's World Phone, and Sprint's International FONCARD. Then, when you're abroad, you call your carrier's local access number. This connects you to a U.S. operator, who places the call for you. This service is invaluable if you don't speak the language. Charges appear on your office phone bill, not your hotel bill. It's good only for calls back to the United States, but you could save up to 40 percent.

Need a cell phone abroad? Taking yours along won't help much because most U.S.-based phones aren't designed to work elsewhere. A few companies offer internationally compatible digital cell phones for rent. Two to call: The Parker Company (800-280-2811) and InTouch USA (800-USA-ROAM).

The right connection

At last count, there were 40 different telephone connectors used worldwide. Even within countries, for example, you can find variations. Saudi Arabia has four different kinds of plugs; Germany has five.

It's a good idea to do some research before you travel. Find out what connectors you'll need and order them. Some hotels, such as Claridges and the Savoy in London, have installed American-compatible RJ-11 phone jacks. Others may follow.

More than 50 percent of the world uses the U.S. RJ-11 plug. To learn which countries use what, visit TeleAdapt's Web site (*www.teleadapt.com*).

To get you started, here's a handy list of a few common destinations and their connection requirements:

CONNECTION REQUIREMENTS

Country	Uses RJ-11?
Australia	
Brazil	
Canada	✔
China	✔
France	
Germany	
Hong Kong	✔
Italy	
Japan	✔
Kenya	
Mexico	✔
Russia	
Saudi Arabia	
South Korea	✔
Switzerland	
Taiwan	
U.K.	

A few countries add metering pulses to their phone signals. They count the high-frequency signals to determine the length of the call. These pulses, also called tax impulsing, definitely slow down modeming and can even cause costly disconnects. You'll encounter tax impulsing in Germany, Switzerland, Austria, Spain, India, Belgium, Slovenia, and the Czech Republic. To overcome the impulses, you'll need a special filter.

When you find it difficult to modem and don't have the right connectors, don't despair. There usually are alternatives. Ask at your hotel; you might be allowed to use the fax line for a few minutes. Almost all fax lines are analog (unless the hotel uses Group IV fax). Ask to use the line late in the evening, after normal business hours, and you may be able to send and receive your e-mail as well.

As a last resort, use public services in the city you're visiting. A good resource is Fodor's Worldview which offers do-it-yourself travel services on the Internet (*www.travelocity.com*). Here you can search a database of information on more than 160 cities. Enter your arrival and departure dates and make selections from a list of such categories as festivals, dining, theater, and hotels. The result: an instant guidebook customized to your specific interests, trip dates, and destinations. You can also learn where to rent a computer, hire a translator, find conference facilities, obtain secretarial services, send a fax, or make a copy.

Recognize this problem?

International dialing

Phone systems around the world use different signals for dial tone, busy, and ringing. Perhaps the strangest busy signal in the world is in Dakar, Senegal, where you'll hear Afro-pop music. Though these strange sounds will not pose a problem when you're dialing a voice call, they will thoroughly confuse your modem. Some modems come with a choice of country configurations. However, many designed to work in the U.S. or Canada may not be able to dial out abroad because they don't recognize the dial tone provided. To get around this, learn how to "blind dial."

How to dial blind

You need to know how to blind dial so that your modem will ignore dial tone. This lets it connect when you're dialing from international locations that produce unrecognizable dial tones. Check your setup file in your modem software. You may be able to select this option. But if your software doesn't allow you to select blind dialing, you can still accomplish it.

1. Change the initialization string in your modem's software. To do this, just add X1 to the end of the string.

2. Disconnect your modem from the phone line.

3. Instruct your modem to tone dial.

4. Listen to your modem. If you hear the series of tones your modem normally makes, you're ready to blind dial.

5. Reconnect your modem to the phone line and dial.

It might be easier to dial manually. Then you don't have to mess around with setup strings and pause length—you just dial as if your modem is a phone. If you don't know how to dial manually, learn. See chapter 5 for more information.

BATTERY BASICS

Batteries are the life force of the itinerant worker. Buy an extra battery or two, keep it charged, and carry it with you. If you don't, you'll kick yourself when you run out of power during that all-important call or when your modem blips out halfway through a crucial download.

Make a habit of battery charging so you won't forget. For instance, get in the routine of doing it immediately upon arrival at your hotel room.

Battery chargers range from small portable trickle chargers to desktop-sized rapid chargers. If your equipment uses nickel-cadmium batteries, get a charger that has a discharge button so you can fully cycle the battery. Otherwise, your battery life will diminish every time you charge.

This is caused by a strange but true phenomenon called battery memory build-up. The cell capacity decreases when batteries are only partially discharged and then recharged. For longer life and less memory loss, get either nickel metal hydride (NiMH) or lithium-ion (LiSB) batteries.

Pack spares

Don't count on automatically finding the battery you need when you need it. Take spares with you. If you're having trouble finding a replacement battery, or your particular model is no longer being produced, you could be in deep trouble. Contact 1-800-Batteries, a discount mail-order company that specializes in batteries for notebooks, laptops, cell phones, and the like (*www.1800batteries.com*).

Warning: *Be careful when packing or toting spare batteries. The acids and heavy metals inside make them unstable. They're prone to electrical mishaps such as shorting out. If they're jolted too much, and if they're sharing a bag with loose metal parts (such as spare change or mini-screwdrivers), an accidental spark could start a fire. Avoid meltdown. Pack safely.*

Harness the sun

How about a solar battery panel installed in your briefcase so you can charge up while taking an alfresco lunch or waiting for a flight? These featherweight solar panels can recharge either from direct sunlight or via indirect artificial lighting. A special plug, similar to a car's cigarette lighter, transfers the stored energy to cell phones, laptops, and other gear. Some cases come with solar panels pre-installed. If you want to add solar capability, contact PowerLine Solar Products (*www.PowerExperts.com*), which manufactures solar panels that work with more than 350 different portable computers.

ROAD WARRIOR'S SURVIVAL KIT

If you plan to connect from anywhere, be sure to pack a toolkit. Stuff to carry:

■ **Modem line tester**

If you use a modem on the road, don't just plug it into any old wall jack. If you run into digital lines, your modem will encounter a higher electrical current over the phone lines than it's designed for. To avoid instant death for your modem, test the line before plugging in.

■ Digital/analog converter

Since analog telephone devices are not compatible with digital lines, you must use modems and other telephone equipment specifically designed for digital lines, or get a converter. Unlimited Systems, Inc. (800-275-6354) offers the best and most complete line of analog/digital converters.

■ Phone plug adapters

If you travel outside the United States, you'll need a variety of devices to adapt to the types of phone plugs you might encounter. TeleAdapt (*www.teleadapt.com*) sells a kit that contains a set of customized foreign telephone plugs, as well as some other handy converters. Magellan's Catalog lists the common plug type needed for 150 countries (*www.magellans.com*).

■ Tone dialer

If you encounter a dial phone (or a phone that looks like a touch-tone phone but doesn't deliver true tones), you'll want a tone dialer. This converts pulse tones into the tones you'll need for accessing such automated phone features as voice mail and bank by phone.

■ Spare parts kit

Keep a shaving kit or small bag pre-packed with spare batteries (wrapped in foam or a cloth bag), a phone line extension cord, three-prong adapter, duo RJ-11 connector, screwdriver, small flashlight, extra diskettes, and the like.

■ Handset coupler

Can't find an RJ-11 plug? Not to worry. Carry a handset coupler (a.k.a. acoustic coupler). It looks like a phone receiver with the ear and mouthpieces replaced by rubber cups. You place your telephone handset into the cups, connect a telephone wire between the coupler and your modem, and dial out. These are especially useful if you travel to a variety of countries, or if you frequently need to connect using a payphone. You can get one capable of transmitting data at up to 24,000 bps, plenty fast.

Real estate agent Eileen Yan uses a handset coupler to download the latest interest rates while writing a property offer at a client's location. Why does she prefer a coupler? "I don't want to ask customers to unplug their phone so I can plug in my fax modem. And it looks pretty undignified if I'm crawling under the furniture searching for a phone jack."

◼ Hot-wiring kit

Some people like to tinker; some don't. I do not recommend this to the faint of heart. However, with the aid of a small screwdriver and a pair of alligator clips, you can get a dial tone without using an RJ-11 connector. To do this, you either remove the cover plate over the phone connection at the wall, or unscrew the telephone mouthpiece. Then you attach clips to the wires, use a testing device to determine which wires carry the phone signal, and attach to your modem. If this kind of activity appeals to you, contact TeleAdapt. They'll set you up with the right tools and a handy instruction manual to boot.

◼ Spare phone cord

Unless you enjoy modeming on the floor or under your bed, you'll want to carry a telephone extension cord. Experts recommend a 25-footer.

◼ Power adapters and plug converters

Most notebook power supplies can sense line voltage changes and automatically switch to the needed power requirements so you no longer have to carry a voltage transformer for your computer. However, if you operate other equipment, you'll want a voltage converter to convert standard U.S. 110-volt power to 220-240-volt power required in most of the rest of the world. Also, be sure to carry the appropriate plug converter so you can plug your machine into the power receptacle.

Argentina
TDPT 261

Argentina
TDPT 262

Australia
TDPT 011

Austria
TDPT 021

Belgium
TDPT 031

Brazil
TDPT 201

Columbia/
Venezuela
TDPT 241

Czech/Slovak
Republic
TDPT 041

Denmark/
Portugal
TDPT 051

Finland/Norway
TDPT 061

France
TDPT 071

Germany
VDO4
TDPT 080

Germany(New)
TAE F
TDPT 081

Germany(Old)
ADOS 4
TDPT 082

Germany
(Former East)
TDPT 084

Germany
ADOS 8
TDPT 086

Greece
TDPT 251

Holland
TDPT 121

Hungary
TDPT 091

India
(UK-Old)
TDPT 271

Isreal (New)
TDPT 221

Isreal(Old)
TDPT 222

Italy (New)
TDPT 101

Italy (Old)
TDPT 103

Iran/Kuwait
Saudi Arabia
TDPT 291

Japan
TDPT 111

Jordan/
Middle East
TDPT 281

Korea/
Saudi Arabia
TDPT 191

Poland/Russia
TDPT 131

Saudi Arabia
TDPT 311

Scandinavia (New)
TDPT 062

South Africa
TDPT 141

Sweden
TDPT 151

Switzerland
(New)
TDPT 161

Switzerland
(Old)
TDPT 162

Turkey
TDPT 211

UK
TDPT 174

USA to UK
TDPT 179

Former
Yugoslavia
TDPT 181

Reprinted with
permission from
TeleAdapt Ltd.
(408) 370-5105

Telephone adapters

MORE TRAVEL TIPS

For more information on international communications, see international faxing in chapter 6.

RESOURCES

Books & magazines
The Business Traveler's Survival Guide: How to Get Work Done While On The Road
by June Langhoff
Aegis Publishing Group, 1997
Full of useful advice, travel planning Web sites, insider tips, real-life stories, and anecdotes. An indispensable travel companion.

Mobile Computing & Communications Magazine
www.mobilecomputing.com

An excellent source of information for the road warrior. Contains frequent reviews of cellular phones, pagers, laptops, and wireless technologies.

On The Road
Robert Lawson, publisher, 802-257-7505
www.roadnews.com

A monthly newsletter for the computer-equipped international traveler. Especially helpful for technology and connection problems.

International callback
International Kallback
800-516-9993
www.kallback.com

Capital Communications of America
800-488-4085
www.ccacorp.com

UCall, I.A.S.
305-937-5118
www.ucall.net

Affinity Telecom
888-988-9024
www.affinitytele.com

Connection tools

Magellan's Catalog
www.magellans.com

TeleAdapt Inc.
www.teleadapt.com

Mobile Planet Inc.
www.mplanet.com

Mobile Office Outfitter
800-426-3453
www.mobilegear.com

CHAPTER 10

Working Together

NOT ALL TELECOMMUTERS ARE LONE WOLVES; many work in teams. Teaming at a distance requires strong communication skills and a system for tracking progress and staying on target. In fact, effective communication is the glue that holds a team together, whether office-based or operating from remote locations. Team members must master a set of skills that allows them to work remotely. Among those skills are:

- Using groupware
- Working in a virtual office
- Getting in sync
- Teaming remotely
- Running and/or attending a teleconference
- Using videoconferencing

USING GROUPWARE

Groupware is software that facilitates teamwork. More than simple group messaging, it is designed to promote information sharing and remote collaboration. Depending on how it's organized, you can set up a workgroup that allows files to be read by everyone in the group, or restrict it to just a few. Some people can be authorized to change files, others just to read them.

Groupware shines when a collaborative project requires lots of coordination. Maybe your team needs to create a report. A draft is composed and posted on an Intranet or groupware site. A message is automatically generated letting all team members know that the draft is available and asking for comments. Each reviewer attaches notes to the document or makes corrections directly. The updates appear in a unique color that identifies a particular group member. Finally, areas of disagreement are ironed out on a teleconference or video-conference with the document in front of everyone on an electronic whiteboard. Changes are made in real time and finalized.

In addition to document conferencing, groupware may also contain capabilities for coordinating group calendars, real-time meetings, workgroup management, knowledge capture, and message forums.

The leaders in the groupware market are Lotus Notes and Lotus Domino (*www.lotus.com*) and Novell's GroupWise (*www.novell.com*).

Two of the most popular office suite software collections also contain some groupware features. Lotus SmarteSuite and MS Office contain the ability to route and track revisions, show updates in different colored inks, embed Internet and Intranet links, and upload presentations to the network.

WORKING IN A VIRTUAL OFFICE

Maybe a dedicated groupware solution is too expensive for your organization but you'd still like to be able to collaborate remotely. A number of companies offer virtual office setups on the Internet. These programs let you set up an Intranet on a private Web site that you rent by the month. Among them are Instant Teamroom (*www.lotus.com*), eRoom (*www.eroom.com*), Involv (*www.involv.com*), and HotOffice (*www.hotoffice.com*).

HotOffice, for example, lets you share files, collaborate online, access documents and e-mail, update a group calendar and contact manager, and work with colleagues by accessing your secure HotOffice Web site using any browser. This solves the problem of working across platforms and makes it easy to work with a team using a number of technologies including Macintoshes, Unix machines, and Windows PCs.

It takes less than an hour to set up an account, and once it's ready, your team can use it to work on common projects, hold online meetings, set up ad hoc bulletin boards, and make group decisions. One feature I think is extra handy is the ability to share applications so that a team can work on the same document in real time and see each other's changes. You can also view documents even if you don't have the correct application on your computer. For example, if a colleague posted an Excel spreadsheet to the Web site, and you didn't have Excel on your computer, you could still view the document by choosing the browser's HTML viewer.

Many organizations use Microsoft NetMeeting (*www.microsoft.com*) as their groupware solution. NetMeeting comes bundled with Internet Explorer or can be downloaded free. NetMeeting lets you share Windows applications such as Excel, Word, or PowerPoint, and edit them cooperatively. By adding a microphone and speakers, you can have real-time telephone conversations over the Net, though you may have to put up with occasional speech delays. NetMeeting even has a videoconferencing capability.

Don Higgins, manager of assembler development at Micro Focus Inc., manages two staff members: one in Palo Alto, California; the other in Newbury, England. Higgins works out of his home near St. Petersburg, Florida. Higgins' group uses Microsoft NetMeeting, which lets them speak to each other real-time, work on shared documents, and use an electronic whiteboard. "This is especially slick for demos," he says.

Macintosh users don't need to feel left out. Many groupware solutions are platform-independent, using a browser interface as the common desktop. Others, such as Timbuktu Pro Conferencing for Macintosh (*www.farallon.com*), have a built-in NetMeeting interface.

TIPS FOR SUCCESSFUL REMOTE TEAMING

Chances are, you'll end up being a member of a number of remote teams. Here's some tips to help make remote collaboration work effectively.

■ **If possible, start with a face-to-face meeting**

The purpose: to get to know each other, identify people's abilities and interests, develop a clear set of agreed-upon goals, and set up a division of labor. Experts suggest that this meeting be led by a professional facilitator, especially for multiorganizational teams where it may be difficult to reach consensus, since no one member has authority to impose a solution.

■ **Spell out roles and responsibilities**

Teams need to develop group objectives and rules about decision making, determine a method for handling disagreements, and form a common understanding of desired outputs.

■ **Develop a common document**

Create a document that states the purpose of the team, identifies the players, specifies delivery dates, and spells out the goals. As you add to it over time, it provides a team history.

■ **Stay sensitive to time zones**

Many teams have members located several time zones away. You need to develop team communication strategies that are sensitive to time zones. Vary the time of your teleconferences or use e-mail more if the times aren't particularly convenient.

■ **Take advantage of time differences**

Fitch, an industrial design consultancy firm with offices in Ohio, was partnering with LG Electronics in Korea. The 12-hour time difference between the two locations would normally have been a hindrance, but working electronically, it became an asset. One team would upload electronic designs, images, and 3-D models at the end of their business day, and the other would download the designs, review them, draw changes, and make decisions before the U.S. contingent came back to work. By collaborating electronically, they were able to finish the product design in record time.

■ Make sure members know how to use group tools

People in intercompany teams may not be running on the same platform. Look for tools that work across platforms such as Internet browsers, Adobe PDF, Framemaker, or Microsoft Office.

■ Vary your communications methods

Try for at least one real-time communications event each week. This could be a teleconference, videoconference, Internet chat or web meeting. Avoid using email or voice mail for emotion-laden issues. When feelings run high, pick up the phone and talk it through.

■ Avoid overcommunicating

Don't copy everyone you know on every e-mail. Learn how to copy and forward mail without sending all the header information. Work on summarizing and simplifying communications. A study of workplace communications conducted by Pitney Bowes Inc. showed that the average corporate worker sends and receives 190 messages a day and many of the e-mails were repetitive. Don't be one of the e-mail abusers.

GETTING IN SYNC

If you use one computer in the office and another at home, you need a surefire method of ensuring that the files you work on at home match the files in the office. One way to do this is to use *sneakernet*. You carry a floppy back and forth between the two computers, and copy the file with the most recent changes over the older file. This is a fine system as long as you remember to do it and you don't have too many files to manage.

Windows 95 & 98 contain a tool called Briefcase that helps you keep your files straight. When you're getting ready to leave the main office, drag the folders you need to use at home onto the Briefcase desktop icon. The next time you're back in the main office, just place the floppy disk containing your Briefcase files into your desktop computer, select the Briefcase, and click Update All.

Norton Mobile Essentials, from Symantec (*www.symantec.com*) offers a bundle of software tools for shuttling files between computers. This program lets you mark all files you need when traveling. Then, the next time you need to take off, you just click a button and everything is copied to your laptop, including contact information, spreadsheets, important files—all automatically. It also has a tool for configuring your computer to particular locations that you visit regularly, including local Internet access numbers, area codes, and even time zones. Then, when you arrive at your destination, click the new city in your list and you're all set.

Many remote access packages contain file synchronization utilities. You just upload the file you need, take it home or on the road, and make your changes. Then you can connect to your LAN remotely, and synchronize the files. These programs operate on the principle of last-modified date. They compare the two versions and overwrite the file with the earlier date. Just make sure that no one in your office changes the file while you're away.

If you want to be sure no one messes with your file while you're gone, mark the office file "read only." Although a determined office mate can override this designation, it will usually keep your files safe until you return.

When two or more people work on the same file, your problems multiply. Since both files may contain valid changes, an update based simply on file date will erase one set of edits. If you encounter this problem, look for a software solution that compares the contents of each file and alerts you when *both* versions of a file have been changed. Possibilities include Traveling Software's LapLink for Windows users (*www.travsoft.com*) or Qdea's Synchronize (*www.qdea.com*) for Macs.

Keeping pocket organizers organized

So now you have your files all nicely synchronized between the office and home computer, but what do you do to make sure that your pocket calendar database matches your computer contact lists? One company that offers a solution is Intellisync (Puma Technology; *www.pumatech.com*). This program can synchronize a Palm Pilot or Windows CE device with Lotus Notes, Novell's GroupWise, Microsoft's Outlook, or Symantec's Act.

Coordinating calendars

Have you ever had to set up a meeting for a bunch of people? You leave a message with the attendees asking when they are free. Then you narrow down the possibilities and leave more messages. You hunt for possible meeting rooms and try to find a time that works for everyone. Several phone calls—and possibly days—later, you've got a date. Now you have to call everyone *again* to notify them of the final meeting plan. Aaargh!

Many online programs can handle this for you. They automate the task by keeping copies of shared calendars, finding open time slots, and securing commitments using e-mailed confirmations. Many programs allow you to read and modify another person's schedule. For example, Schedule Online (*www.scheduleonline.com*) allows you to schedule meetings, tasks, and even to-do items. If you want to set up a meeting, you list the members you'd like to attend and the software takes over. It automatically checks the schedules of all invitees, spots conflicts, and lets you view members' calendars so you can identify potential time slots. It compiles a list of attendees and can even send reminder e-mails. Other online calendar sites include Visto Briefcase (*www.visto.com*), Jump! (*www.jump.com*), and Yahoo! Calendar (*calendar.yahoo.com*).

TELECONFERENCING

Need to meet with far-flung colleagues, yet avoid travel costs? Schedule a teleconference with your phone company or with a teleconference service bureau. Compared to the cost of business travel, teleconferences are an attractive alternative.

According to a 1998 survey of business travel by Runzheimer International, a domestic three-day business trip averages $1,037 and the cost of an average seven-day international trip is $3,542. Compare that to a one-hour teleconference. A dozen participants located around the country can meet for an hour for around $200. If they all flew in for the meeting (and none stayed overnight), that same meeting would cost around $6,000.

Types of teleconference services

Conferencing services offer a variety of conference-calling options. Here are some of the most common:

- **Meet-me number:** Callers call a preassigned telephone number and pay for their own long-distance call charges. There is no on-call operator or automated announcements. Meet-me calls take a bit of getting used to—if you're the first person to call in, you hear nothing until someone else joins you on the line. If participants are not briefed, they may hang up. I know I did the first time I encountered one of these lines. So brief all parties about how it works and insist on promptness. This type of service works best for small meetings.

- **Automated service:** Like meet-me numbers, callers pay for their own long-distance call charges. After dialing in to the preassigned number, they are greeted by an automated voice and prompted to announce themselves. Callers are then automatically placed into the conference call. Operator assistance is available, often by pressing zero. This type of call is recommended for smaller groups where people know each other.

- **Operator-assisted call:** Callers dial a toll-free number. The call is answered by a human being, and the caller is placed in a hold queue until the conference begins. The assistant might take roll, control the question and answer session, or help with offline technical questions. You can also arrange for a tape or transcript of the call, which is extra handy if you need to keep comprehensive notes or minutes. This type of service works best for calls with large numbers of participants, and especially for calls where everyone is not already acquainted.

■ **Advanced services**: Conferencing companies are adding lots of special services to enhance the call, such as the ability to upload and display PowerPoint slides on a Web site, electronic whiteboarding services, or document collaboration services.

Scheduling a call

To locate a teleconferencing services company, call your local telephone company or look in the Yellow Pages under Tele-conference Services. Major national companies include: AT&T (800-232-1234), The Conference Center (800-825-2578), Confertech (800-525-8244), MCIWorldCom (800-475-5000), and Sprint (800-366-2663).

You'll need to specify the number of ports (phone lines you need), the date and time of the call, and the services you require. Then send your agenda to everyone in sufficient time and make sure they all know how to use the service you've selected. Send an e-mail or fax with the most important particulars: phone number to dial, time and date of the call (if in different time zones, list each or specify the host time zone), call duration, conference name, host name, and, if required, password.

A word about speakerphones

Participants who are sharing a phone line may gather in someone's office and listen in by speakerphone. If your group does this, make sure that you have a quality speakerphone. Test it out in advance. You want to be sure it doesn't clip conversations when another person is speaking. This will happen if the phone has a half-duplex microphone, typical of standard speakerphones. Such phones pick up all sorts of sounds and can create echoes and reverbs. Make sure the phone you're using has a full-duplex mike or even better, a conferencing phone. This is a special phone set with a number of microphones for 360° sound pickup, special processors to cancel out echoes, and automatic gain control so that quiet talkers can be heard.

Quality speakerphones are rated for the number of people they're designed to support. They also come in a variety of configurations to accommodate various room sizes. A triangular-shaped phone with mikes in each angle will normally handle up to 10 people and a room size up to 20 x 24. Anything larger will require a speakerphone with extension mikes.

For the best sound quality, use the speakerphone in a room with curtains and a carpet. Place the phone on a wooden surface, not on metal or glass. If your conference tabletop is glass, put the phone on a telephone book or other sound cushioner.

Running a teleconference

A successful conference call requires a bit of planning and management. If you're hosting the call, follow these steps to make your teleconference a success:

- Fax or e-mail an agenda in advance. That way, participants can come prepared.

- If you need to review printed materials during the call, make sure everyone has a copy in advance.

- During the call, strive to include everyone by asking for opinions. Otherwise, it's easy for members of your audience to zone out or feel unneeded.

- Help people stay on target. If you have a free-wheeling discussion, always guide participants back to the agenda.

- Make a note of any new topics that come up and schedule them for your next meeting.

- Stick to your time limit.

- At the end, thank everyone.

- Record the meeting, type up your notes, and send out a summary to each participant.

Nortel's Ian Norman, telecommuting services manager for Europe, notes that people need to learn how to effectively manage audio calls. He recommends advanced preparation, polling everyone for their opinion, and working out the niceties of the beginning of the call. "We sometimes spend 10 minutes saying hello to everybody and then end up with too little time to get through all the material," says Norman. So skip the small talk and get to business sooner.

Attending a teleconference

Teleconferencing is easy as long as you follow a few simple guidelines:

- Deactivate Call Waiting before dialing in.
- The conference manager will give you a toll-free number to call and possibly a PIN code. Write them down where you can find them easily.
- If you're expecting packages, leave a note for any delivery people instructing them to drop items off without your signature.

- Be on time. Dial in a couple of minutes before the conference is scheduled to begin.

- Put your phone on Mute. If you don't, others may be able to hear noises in your office from up to 40 feet away. This can cause the audio signal to break up. It is also highly distracting.

- If you want to ask a question, wait until the moderator calls for them. Usually, you will be required to enter a code on your telephone keypad to indicate that you have a question or comment.

- When you speak, don't expect people to figure out who you are. Identify yourself every time.

- Never use your speakerphone when asking a questions or addressing the group. Otherwise, you'll sound imperious—as well as garbled or distorted.

- Some conference calls are real snores. If you find yourself losing attention, put the conference on speakerphone and do something quiet to wake yourself up. I open my mail or balance my checkbook. If I get really sleepy, I do stretches.

WEB CONFERENCING

The Web is becoming a virtual meetingplace for many workgroups. Specialized Internet sites let you host meetings for large numbers of attendees, display Microsoft PowerPoint slide shows, even allow the audience to interact with the speakers. PlaceWare Conference Center (*www.placeware.com*), for example, provides a virtual auditorium with streaming audio and video, interactive audience polls, and question and answer capabilities. Other conferencing sites include RealNetwork's G2 (*www.real.com*) and Contigo's Internet Conference Center (*www.contigo.com*). Many organizations use Web conferencing to conduct remote training sessions.

You can hold small meetings or set up an online forum or community on free sites such as PowWow (*www.tribal.com*), eGroups (*www.eGroups.com*), and Forum One (*www.-forumone.com*). These programs include a number of features that are useful for remote workgroups. For example, PowWow offers group chat, voice chat, instant messages, buddy lists, text to voice, Web tours, bulletin board, and limited whiteboarding.

Some companies use online instant-messaging programs, such as ICQ and AOL's Instant Messenger, to keep teams in touch. These programs will display messages on your desktop to let you know that a member of your group wants to communicate with you real time. Some programs will let you run instant messaging as a background application, setting it to "answering machine" mode so you're not disturbed.

VIDEOCONFERENCING

PC-based videoconferencing is perfect for situations that require demonstrations or face-to-face meetings. Desktop video is being used by companies to cut down on the amount of travel required.

The setup usually consists of a small camera mounted on top of a monitor, one or more video adapter cards for the computer, software to run the program, a microphone and speaker, or telephone handset. The software usually comes with some kind of shared whiteboard or document collaboration software. When a video conference is in session, the two computers are connected via a standard analog telephone line or an ISDN line.

Most systems support point-to-point teleconferences, limiting the conference to two computers. To set up a conference, simply launch the video software and dial the other PC by clicking on a photo in your graphical phone book. Then start the software you want to view, seat yourself before the tiny video camera, and you're on stage. Your image (usually just head and shoulders) appears in a small box on the other screen. Add a document camera, and you can share drawings, charts, graphics, and 3-D objects.

Some desktop video programs run on ordinary analog lines; others require ISDN lines. The video quality on analog lines is often poor, with fuzzy images, jerky action, and delayed audio. That's because most analog connections support only about five frames a second (versus 30 on your TV). ISDN connections double or triple the speed to between 10 and 15 frames per second. The better video systems combine three ISDN lines for full-motion video quality.

Bill Holtz, a vice president with Nortel, telecommutes daily from his home outside Philadelphia to his office in Texas. Using a videoconferencing facility he installed in his basement, Holtz converses with staff and customers around the world. He cut his travel miles to the bone by replacing travel with video meetings. His videoconference setup costs about 30¢ a minute to operate. With this setup, according to Holtz, "distance no longer matters." When he needs to conference with a customer who doesn't have in-house video capability, his staff helps the customer locate the nearest public video center and sets up an appointment. When it's time for the meeting, Holtz heads downstairs, aims the camera at his face, and logs on. It's that simple.

If you don't have desktop video capability, but need to conduct an occasional videoconference, consider renting. Some office support companies and teleworking centers offer videoconferencing facilities. For example, Kinko's copy centers (800-743-2679) provide room-based videoconferencing at many of their branches at affordable rates. Expect to pay about $150 for a one-hour, two-site meeting.

Want to videoconference with your team or attend a long-distance training class? Check out group videoconferencing services. Each person dials into a toll-free number to join the videoconference. Participants can even dial in from a standard telephone for a voice-only connection. Works worldwide—anywhere there's an ISDN phone line. For information, contact Pacific Bell (800-WE MEET U), Sprint (800-669-1235), Connexus (800-938-8888), and MCIWorldCom (800-475-5000).

Attending a videoconference

Here are some tips to help you survive your first videoconference:

- Find out what you're supposed to look at. If you're having a one-on-one desktop videoconference, look directly at the camera when you're speaking to the person on the other end of the connection.

- Don't worry excessively about your appearance. Almost everyone looks weird on desktop video. Skin tones are often greenish; colors are frequently washed out.

- Wear neutral colors but avoid white or light blue. Stay away from small prints or stripes.

- To improve your transmitted picture quality and color, turn on all the lights, even in the daytime.

- Stay loose. Try to look as if you're enjoying what you're doing.

- Because there is a built-in delay between the time when you say something and your audience hears it (can be up to 30 seconds), pause before starting to speak. Otherwise, you may end up verbally stepping on the previous speaker.

- Keep fast movements to a minimum. Because desktop video runs over phone lines, it doesn't have the bandwidth to handle rapid movement and images will tend to be blurred. Attempt to keep your head and hands still without looking stiff.

RESOURCES

Books

Cybermeetings: How to Link People and Technology in Your Organization
by James Creighton & James Adams
Amacom, 1998

Virtual Teams: Reaching Across Space, Time, and Organizations With Technology
by Jessica Lipnack & Jeffrey Stamps
John Wiley & Sons, 1997

Managing Virtual Teams: Techniques for High-Technology Project Managers
by Martha Haywood
Artech Horizon House, 1998

CHAPTER 11

Safeguarding Your Work

YOU SHOULD PRACTICE good computer habits whether you're at home, on the road, or in the office. However, because telecommuters often use more than one computer and may work in several potentially unsecured areas, they increase their exposure to risk. Also, if you work with highly confidential information, you'll need to take additional security precautions. So put your mind at ease, and help your company's network manager relax by practicing extra safe computer behavior.

This chapter provides some tips for safeguarding your work and includes a section on special security measures for working on the road.

PROTECT WITH PASSWORDS

At the very least, you should protect your system with a log-on password. If you share a computer with family members, protect the directories (or folders) you use with a folder locking program such as FolderBolt (*www.citadel.com*) or Norton DiskLock (*www.symantec.com*). Such programs will prevent accidental erasures or overwriting of files. One telecommuter reported that his five-year-old son erased his entire hard drive by playing a game that involved moving file icons into "this neat trash can."

Use long, hard-to-crack passwords; change them often. Some computer hackers program their systems to try every word in their computerized dictionaries in an attempt to break in. So don't use words that are found in a dictionary, or if you do, combine them. Odd word combinations or nonsense known only to you are good possibilities.

Bad passwords

Bad passwords include birthdays, Social Security numbers, phone numbers, names of family members, pets, and simple words, such as:

- 12/7/54
- Rover
- 547-33-1257

Good passwords

Good passwords are nonsense words, combinations of words and symbols, and long strings, such as:

- 5Vaderforawith
- %*@9914afuzz
- tiddlytumtu

Experts say not to write your passwords down. Well, fine! What do those of us with memories already overflowing with information do? If you're like me, you've got a multitude of passwords and PINs to remember: your bank ATM card, phone card, online services, Internet access, Web site passcodes, as well as corporate log-ins for a variety of programs and files. How can you keep track of them all? Write your passwords down but keep them in an out-of-the-ordinary place. Don't keep them in your office, on a calendar, or in a computer file. (I'm not telling where I keep mine.) Whatever you do, don't put passwords on a Post-it note attached to your computer screen. And avoid using the same password for all systems.

Another alternative is to get your company to install a log-in authentication security system. This is a combination of software installed on your LAN's server and a log-in card about the size of a credit card, for each user. The system randomly generates a password and changes it every 60 seconds. You use the password that appears on your card when logging into the corporate system. Works like a charm—as long as you don't lose the card. For more information, contact Security Dynamics and ask about its SecureID card (*www.securitydynamics.com*).

Hate passwords? There are secure alternatives. You could unlock files by speaking to your computer through a microphone. The system compares your voice to a stored voice print before allowing you access (VoiceCrypt, *www.voicecrypt.com*). Mount a video camera and show your face when you want to log on (True Face PC, *www.miros.com*). Or use your finger or thumbprints to identify yourself (U.are.U., *www.digitalpersona.com*). Using technologies developed originally for secret agents, solutions using biometrics are finally affordable. You can avoid passwords (at least some of them) for around $100.

ENCRYPT YOUR DATA

If you travel on the job or carry highly sensitive information, you should use a data encryption system. The encryption software converts your file into an unreadable mess that can only be read with the aid of a *key* that decodes the file. Use a program such as PGP (Pretty Good Privacy; *www.nai.com*) or Norton's Your Eyes Only (*www.symantec.com*). You can encrypt any kind of file: spreadsheet, database, text, or graphics.

Encryption works well as long as you're the owner of the data and know the key to unlock the information. It gets trickier if you want to send an encrypted file to someone else. To send a secure file, you encrypt it but you still need to tell the recipient how to decrypt the file. You could call and provide the key over the phone or mail it—but each of these carries an additional security risk. You're already worried about spies gleaning company secrets from your files, think how bad it would be to give them the entire key to your coding scheme! A special type of encryption has been developed to handle this problem. It's called public-key cryptography. Here's how it works:

I want to send a file to Jane Doe. I encrypt my file using Jane's public key, which she makes available to anyone who asks. When the file reaches her, she decrypts the message using her private key, known only to her.

Think of this as two locks—one with a passkey that everyone who needs it has, and one with a special key accessible to only one person. Both keys are required to access the message.

ERADICATE YOUR FILES

Did you know that when you delete a file from your hard disk, it doesn't *really* get erased? Your computer just scrubs the file's name off your directory and makes a mental note that the space that file occupied is now available for reassignment. The file doesn't disappear until the disk sector it occupied gets overwritten, days or even weeks later.

This fact is well-known to computer thieves and other sneaky types bent on obtaining company secrets. Once again, if your files are supposed to be top secret, you'll need to be sure that they are erased completely. Look for security software that offers electronic paper shredding or *incineration* capability such as FolderBolt (*www.citadel.com*).

KEEP YOUR PORTS CLOSED

If you use a cable modem for Internet access, you join a local area network (LAN) with other cable users in your neighborhood. This can cause problems, especially if someone wants to snoop in your files. Make sure that no one can gain access by turning off file sharing capability in your computer. Here's how:

- ■ **Windows:** In the Network Control Panel, click Configuration, then select File and Print Sharing. Deselect the radio button next to "I want to be able to give others access to my files." Click OK twice.

- ■ **Macintosh:** In the File Sharing Control Panel, check to see that "File Sharing is Off" and for a button marked

"Start." If you see a button marked "Stop," click on it. You'll be asked how many minutes the computer should wait until it turns file sharing off. Select a number and click OK.

STAY VIGILANT ABOUT VIRUSES

A computer virus is a software program designed to disrupt computer processing. Many computer users spread viruses without knowing it.

According to the *Antivirus Researcher's Report*, 200 new viruses appear each month. Your computer could get infected with a virus if you run a program that is infected or even if you open an e-mail attachment that contains a virus. You can get infected files from all sorts of places:

■ Programs downloaded from bulletin boards, the Internet, and other online sources

■ Files you've copied from a friend's floppy or hard disk

■ Brand-new commercial software

■ Executable files attached to e-mail messages

Pirated software often carries viruses. According to a recent *InfoWorld* survey, 97.6 percent of all the computers in China have been infected by a virus. The high percentage of infection is attributed to the amount of software piracy and illegal copying of software that goes on in that country.

Your first step in protection is to get a virus protection program and use it regularly. See *Resources* for anti-virus software contact information.

Avoid e-mail flu

Attachments sometimes carry diseases. You can get a macro virus by opening and saving an infected Microsoft document attached to an e-mail. Infections have been found in most of the Office suite programs including Access, Word, PowerPoint, and Excel. Once a macro virus gets onto your machine, it can spread to all future documents you create with the application.

Another strain of viruses invade your computer address book, steal a bunch of e-mail addresses, and send out loads of copies of an e-mail that appear to come from you. Sort of like a chain letter on speed.

There's also concern about a virus that infects HTML-enabled e-mail programs. It works like this: Destructive HTML code is enclosed in a message as a standard URL link. If you click on the link, it triggers a program to run.

If you receive an e-mailed attachment from someone you don't know, don't open it. Send it to the trash or recycle bin. And always use protection in the form of an anti-virus program.

Use it or lose it

Remember, any program you use is only effective recognizing known viruses. You must keep your program current by downloading new search strings (which you can download from your software vendor's Web site) that help you detect new viruses. Also subscribe to regular program updates so that you can safely remove infected programs.

Recognize the symptoms of infection

There are all kinds of viruses. Some can remain hidden in your system for months or even years. Each virus exhibits different symptoms. Here are some clues:

- Your computer's date and time stamps change mysteriously.
- You find yourself running out of disk space because your programs are growing in size.
- Your system experiences frequent crashes.
- Your computer is slowing down.
- You get strange or silly error messages such as "Feed me" or "Happy Birthday, Ludwig."
- Your disk is erased automatically.

Steps for avoiding infection

■ Keep your anti-virus program current by subscribing to the program's update service, which sends you new search-and-repair routines. Think of them as inoculations.

■ Don't download programs (or files with attached programs) from bulletin boards or Web sites not well known to you.

■ Never buy or use pirated software.

■ If you do download a file, check for viruses before using.

■ If you receive e-mail with an attached file from an unknown source, don't open the attached file. Promptly erase it.

■ Avoid installing software if the package is damaged or shows signs of tampering.

■ Back up your hard disk frequently.

POWER PROBLEMS

Running on home power lines may increase the risk of power outages and spikes that may affect your equipment and/or data. And lightning protection may not be as effective on your home system as it is in the office. Even something as mundane as a home hair-dryer or electric pencil sharpener can draw excessive current that harms computers and other home office equipment. In fact, a study by IBM showed that a typical computer is subject to more than 120 power problems per month.

With so many potential power risks, how can teleworkers cope? Here are some suggestions that may help you weather the next storm.

Suppress surges

Electricity is variable and the effects of uneven power are often invisible. A slight dip or surge in power may not shut off your system but can, over time, produce data errors and add wear and tear on your hard drive. Power fluctuations can also introduce line noise that causes "snow" on computer monitors, increased data glitches, and reduced hard drive life.

The simplest way to iron out the power peaks and valleys is to place a surge protector between your equipment and outside power. A good surge protector will be able to handle at least 400 *joules* (the amount of energy the device can absorb). Make sure that the device carries an Underwriter Laboratories Voltage Let-through rating of 400 or lower. Also look for a UL 1449 rating to ensure that the equipment is built to withstand lightning hits.

Make sure that all networked equipment is protected. If a printer or scanner is not plugged into a surge suppressor, and is connected to your network, it can serve as an electrical conductor in the event of a lightning strike. The unhappy result: everything fries.

Upgrade to UPS

Surge protectors are good insurance but won't keep your computer running when the power goes out. If you live in an area with severe windstorms, chronic brownouts, or lightning storms, consider getting an uninterruptible power supply (UPS). A UPS provides backup power to keep your computer and peripherals running for a period of time, ranging from about five minutes to more than an hour. The idea is to give you sufficient time to save your work and power down your system safely.

There are many factors to consider when selecting a UPS system. The most important:

- **Power rating:** This is expressed in volt-amperes (VA) and represents the output capacity of a UPS.

- **Output factor:** Most UPSs have an output factor of .6 or .7. To determine what kind of output you'll get, multiply VA by the output factor. Thus, a 500VA machine with an output factor of .7 will yield 350 watts.

- **Run time:** This is the length of time the unit will provide AC power while operating on its battery. Run times of five to 15 minutes are most common for units in the

$150 to $300 range. Equipment with longer running times will cost more.

■ **Current draw:** This is the total amps that a unit can support. You need to check the amperage needs of your equipment and make sure that the total doesn't exceed the specs on the UPS. If you have a UPS with a current draw of 4.2 amps, for example, and plug in a laser printer that draws 5 amps, you risk overloading and damaging the UPS.

■ **Warranty:** Make sure that the warranty covers the replacement of your equipment if it fails when protected by the UPS. If you have more than one UPS in your office, be sure that they are all made by the same company. Otherwise, the companies may argue about who is at fault, and you may end up with no compensation.

Get off the grid

To cope with a long-term power failure, some use a portable gasoline or diesel generator. Be sure to operate the generator in a sheltered, well-ventilated area such as a garage or porch. Generally speaking, the generator should have three times the wattage of the equipment that would run on backup power. For example, a 1.5-kilowatt generator can power your computer, portable telephone, and a couple of lamps.

Sun power is another option. You can get a fold-out solar charger that's powerful enough to run a notebook computer for around $400. The Sun Catcher (PowerLine Solar Products, *www.powerexperts.com*) can fit inside a laptop portfolio, powering Macs, PCs, satellite phones, digital cameras—anything that you could normally plug into your auto's cigarette lighter socket.

Defeat lightning

Though most telecommuters protect against electrical surges, many do not protect their equipment from lightning strikes. You may not be aware that lightning can travel over phone lines, Web TV, or pay-per-view lines; through your modem;

and zap your computer. That's what happened to Kerri McBride's equipment when lightning struck near her home. Her surge protectors were undamaged. However, she says: "I had a dead PC (motherboard, fax card, sound card, scanner card, and blown, unrecoverable hard drive) *and* a dead color deskjet, three dead phones, two dead TVs—not to mention a cooked microwave."

Since that day, McBride has become a surge suppressor expert. Her advice:

- Judge your surge protector by the value of the warranty guarantee. Don't buy one that doesn't cover the replacement of your system.

- Buy all your surge protectors from the same manufacturer. That way no one will argue about whose was the bad guy if a surge protector fails.

- Be sure you have computer hardware insurance. Know what the deductible is and what is covered.

- Check the policies of equipment still under warranty. Many companies won't replace items damaged by "acts of God."

- Use surge protectors with RJ-11 jacks for your phones and fax lines.

Even surge protectors may not protect you from a direct hit. You should physically unplug all equipment from the wall (including your phones) if you find yourself in the eye of a thunderstorm. Don't plug back in until the lightning strikes are at least a second (1,000 feet) away.

If you travel, be sure to ask if your hotel has protected phone lines. Mike Irwin, CFO of Wild Planet Toys, learned this lesson the hard way. On a recent trip to England, he was working in his hotel room downloading files when his modem blew. The culprit: a power surge traveling through the phone lines.

DISASTER-PROOF YOUR HOME OFFICE

Disasters come in all sizes and varieties—from localized catastrophes such as fires and broken water mains to such regional disasters as floods, earthquakes, blizzards, and high winds. Not all disasters are caused by Mother Nature. Sometimes humans are at fault, as with strikes, civil disturbances, and sabotage. There are also systems failures such as power spikes and outages, toxic spills, cut cables, and leaky pipes.

As a telecommuter, you can help your company out when disaster strikes. Because you're equipped to operate remotely, you'll keep the business in motion until the main office can reopen. For example, telecommuters, armed with laptops and cellular phones, managed to publish *Mobile Office* magazine even though the head office was crippled by the Northridge earthquake.

Telecommuters need to be prepared for any eventuality. Here are some tips to follow:

- Take a copy of your company's disaster plan home with you. That way, if disaster strikes, you'll know who to contact and how to stay in touch with your office-mates.

- Use an online service, such as AOL or CompuServe, as a backup communications link in an emergency. That way, if your office e-mail is down, you can still communicate.

- If you live in earthquake country, be sure that tall bookcases and heavy file cabinets are attached to the walls. Invest in safety straps to secure your computer and other heavy equipment to your desk.

- Don't rely on cordless phones alone. They need electrical power in order to operate—tough luck in a brownout or grid failure. Keep a corded phone for emergencies.

- Make sure all your surge protectors are certified by the Underwriter's Laboratory and have sufficient jacks for phone and modem lines.

- Store copies of your backup files offsite. Mail floppies to your office; send backups via modem to your LAN or an Internet storage site.

- Keep a fire extinguisher in your home office. Install smoke-heat detectors, too. Test the smoke detectors on a weekly basis.

Fire Captain John La Bounty of the Conneaut, Ohio Fire Department warns that fire-proof safes aren't all that reliable. "It's not the fire that damages the materials inside," he says, "but the heat. I have seen people open a safe after a fire is out, and watch the papers crumble in their hand." La Bounty advises using a bank safe deposit box for important papers. Barring that, store your safe in the basement or an area that is least likely to be exposed to high temperatures.

BACKUP FREQUENTLY

Probably the best step you can take is to back up your files regularly. According to Mich Kabay, author of *The NCSA Guide to Enterprise Security* (McGraw-Hill, 1995), many back up their computers daily, but then make the mistake of leaving their current backup tape or disk right next to the computer they're trying to protect. This is obviously a poor solution. If the computer gets stolen, melted, or drowned, so will the backup. Kabay recommends leaving your backup files with a friendly neighbor. "Failing that," he says, "if your nearest neighbor is miles away or is a grump—at least put the tapes in a fire-resistant safe as far from the computer as possible."

Now that computer files are so huge and disk drives are in the gigabit range, it can take hours to back up files. Not only that, you'd need more than 2,500 diskettes to back up a 4-gig system. Many teleworkers back up to tape, cartridge, or a removable drive, such as a Zip or Jaz drive, to simplify the task. Others back up to their company LAN via a software program such as pcTelecommute (*www.symantec.com*) or LapLink (*www.travsoft.com*). Another solution is Internet backup, such as SafeGuard (*www.sgii.com*), Connected Online (*www.connected.com*), or @Backup (*www.atbackup.com*). These companies store your backups in secure vaults, will back up your files automatically (if you so desire), and can send you a CD-ROM of your entire system, all for a monthly fee.

GUARD AGAINST ESPIONAGE

This may sound like cloak-and-dagger stuff to you, but there is a class of criminal that preys on traveling businesspeople, remote workers, and telecommuters. You need to stay alert to foil them.

- Put a lock on the telephone access box outside your home. This will guard against vandalism, wire-tapping, and pirated long-distance calls. If you don't lock it, anyone with a modular phone can plug in, listen to your calls, or make a few of their own.

- Don't work where someone can see your computer screen through the window. According to security experts, an industrial spy can lift company secrets by photographing screenfuls of information using a high-powered lens from 100 feet away.

- Guard your trash. Garbage belongs to anyone. The United States Supreme Court has ruled that once trash is put out for collection, it is no longer private property. It can be studied, kept, and used as evidence in court. Shred those papers or take them back to the office for disposal.

- Don't get in the habit of leaving your PC powered on when you leave. If you don't turn it off, you make it too easy for others to pick your computer's brain.

- If you have an "always-on" Internet connection, such as cable or DSL, turn it off when you're not there. Otherwise, you may open a backdoor to your files, or worse yet, to your company LAN.

- Use a cordless phone with a system that scrambles the voice signal, preventing electronic eavesdropping and ensuring privacy. Then if someone listens in, all he'll hear is garbled speech.

- If your modem shares a line with a cordless phone, unplug the phone before sending e-mail or an encrypted file.

SECURITY TIPS FOR WORKING ON THE ROAD

Data is valuable. How valuable can be attested by a news item reported in *Business Week* in 1999: John Kauza, a security expert at AT&T, described why industrial spies are interested in traveling executives: "I can get $3,000 for a top-of-the-line laptop," he said, "but I can get a million to a million-and-a-half dollars for your marketing plans." Though you may not tote around as many company secrets, you still have a great deal to lose if your portable gets purloined.

According to industry studies, laptop theft was the second-most prevalent computer crime in 1998 (computer viruses took first place). The FBI reported more than 300,000 laptop thefts of which 90 percent are never recovered due to a black market for spare parts. Cellular fraud costs another $1 million a day.

Here are some steps to take to keep you from being a victim:

- If your calls are sensitive and must be secure, avoid cellular phones. For the same reason, don't give out your credit card numbers over cell phones.

- Be on the lookout for signs of cellular fraud, and especially for lurking phone cloners.

- If you tend to carry your laptop around without a case, attach some grippy tape to the back of your machine so it is less likely to slip out of your hands and crash on the tarmac.

- Treat your laptop to the same degree of parental anxiety you'd show to a two-year-old toddler. Don't leave it unattended, even for an instant.

- Don't leave your laptop alone in a hotel room, either. Arrange to lock it up in the hotel safe. Barring that, carry a portable lock and steel cable and chain it to something really heavy. Kensington Technology makes a range of excellent locking products (*www.kensington.com*).

- Install a device that locks up your laptop such as the Data Defender (*www.lapjack.com*), which provides a unique key that you insert in a parallel port before you can boot up the system.

- Add an alarm that sounds off when your laptop moves. A bunch of companies make motion-activated alarms for mobile computers. Check out Defcon (*www.port.com*), TrackIt (*www.trackitcorp.com*), and Innovative Security Products (*www.wesure.com*).

▪ Install tracking software such as CompuTrace (*www.computrace.com*) or CyberAngel (*www.sentryinc.com*). The software traces the call if and when the thief next connects the modem to a phone line. CompuTrace maintains that its software can pinpoint the location of the missing laptop within 14 seconds of the call. They then contact the police and tell them where the computer is.

▪ The best defense for your data is a time-honored technique: split it up. Carry your programs on your laptop. Carry your data in a removable hard disk, on a PC card in your shirt pocket, or on a few floppies tucked inside your briefcase. And be sure to erase the files on your hard disk using an incineration program (see "Eradicate your files" in this chapter).

INSURANCE—YOUR FINAL BACKUP

Some insurance policies include home office equipment; others don't. Be sure to check with your insurance provider to get the details about your coverage. Many standard homeowners policies include $5,000 protection for loss of computer hardware and software. If the equipment you use is owned by your parent company, and you're just borrowing it while using it at home, your company's insurance should cover any loss incurred at home.

If your insurance policy doesn't cover computer equipment losses, or the coverage contains too many stipulations (such as non-coverage while in transit), consider getting special insurance. SafeWare (*www.safeware-ins.com*), a national insurance company, specializes in computers. Its standard policy provides for full replacement of equipment and software lost through fire, theft, power surges, vandalism, accident, and most natural disasters.

RESOURCES

Anti-virus software

Norton AntiVirus
Symantec
www.symantec.com

PC-cillin
Trend Software
www.antivirus.com

ViruScan
McAfee Associates
www.mcafee.com

Web sites

International Computer Security Association Forum
www.icsa.net

CHAPTER 12

Troubleshooting

AS A TELECOMMUTER, you're expected to be able to handle many of life's little computer emergencies and communication glitches on your own. One of the tradeoffs for the freedom and flexibility of working at home is that you'll need to provide some of your own technical support. Become proficient with your software. Read the technical manuals that come with your hardware and software. Learn to diagnose and solve problems. And finally, learn to recognize when you need help and how to get it. This chapter will help.

Things go wrong. And often, they go wrong at the worst possible time. Computers and other electronic equipment seem to know when you're in a hurry or past a deadline. *Washington Post* columnist Mary McGrory once remarked, "My nephew Edward says machines are like dogs—they can sense when you don't like them."

Technical breakdowns plague everyone who uses computer equipment but the ramifications are worse for those of us who work from home. Telecommuters are especially vulnerable for a couple of reasons:

1. They want to keep their productivity high so that their company will continue to allow them to work from home.

2. Many companies do not assist them in becoming techno-savvy—their employers just expect them to cope as best they can or come back to the office to work.

Getting help for software and hardware problems is one of the most difficult problems telecommuters face. According to a survey of *PCWorld* readers, more than half of the respondents reported problems with their computers. Though the time waiting on a help queue was not excessive (average 10.5 minutes), it took an average of 26 hours to reach a support person who could actually help. It gets worse. A week was the average time spent before the problem was fixed. When your computer is crucial to your worklife, you can't afford to wait.

You need to become techno-savvy if you want to work remotely. Although you're not required to solve every computer mystery, you must be able to cope with common problems. And it's much easier to do so if you're prepared.

COMPUTER CATASTROPHES

Computer problems come in a bewildering variety. Trouble with a memory module, interface board, or disk drive might knock your computer down. Faulty cables, loose expansion cards, software viruses or program conflicts can stop you cold. If your system appears dead, don't despair. It may just be pretending.

Diagnosing the problem

While I can't give you instructions for handling every kind of equipment and software crisis you might experience, there are some common-sense steps that will help you isolate the problem.

1. Turn the power off and then on again. Strange but true, this often works.

2. Check your cables and power cords. Over time they can wriggle free. Occasionally, my mouse appears to die. No matter where I click, I get no action. Before I shut down the system and start up again, I check the mouse cord. Sure enough—the connection is loose.

3. Write down exactly what you were doing when the problem occurred. This is useful for a couple of reasons: 1) it helps you analyze the problem; 2) it keeps the information fresh for conferring with tech support.

4. Print out or copy any error message you see and look it up in your manual. You might be surprised to find the answer to your problem. According to industry analysts, more than half of all tech support problems can be solved by looking in the manuals that come with the equipment or software. You may actually save time by checking the table of contents and the troubleshooting index in your manual. There may also be additional troubleshooting help in the help files preinstalled on your hard disk (that is, if you can get your computer running so you can look there).

5. Try to duplicate the problem. If this suggestion scares you, you don't know enough about the problem yet. Repeat steps 2 through 4.

6. Get help. See below.

Whoops! Dealing with accidental erasures

It happens to the best of us—you're working at breakneck speed to get a project done, copying files, multitasking like mad. You're sure you no longer need that file—and you need more room on your hard drive—so you erase it. Then you realize you goofed and need that file back—and in a hurry, too.

Time to break out your utility program. Hopefully you've already installed it on your hard disk. Using the utility, you can recover at least part of your file. And, if you didn't do any more computing after you erased the file, you may be able to recover the whole thing. If you don't have any utilities, pick up a suite of useful tools such as Symantec's Norton Utilities (*www.symantec.com*).

A truck ran over my laptop!

Don't assume that if you can't recover the files using your utility program, all is lost. Your last line of attack is to send your damaged disk, ruptured laptop, or hammered hard drive to a data retrieval expert. You can find such experts in the *Yellow Pages* under Computer Service & Repairs.

Experts in data recovery tell hair-raising tales of data rescue and claim to be able to recover up to 90 percent of the damaged data they work on. These include computers that have been dropped out of a three-story window, run over by a bus, torched in a car fire, even lost overboard. Pray nothing so terrible happens to you, but if it does, try one of these services:

- ■ DriveSavers (800-440-1904; *www.drivesavers.com*)
- ■ Total Recall (800-743-0594; *www.totalrecall.com*)

Other disk-asters

Disk drives are the weak link in most computer systems. They wear out. Unfortunately, they don't tell you when. They just die one day—usually when they're needed the most.

When you turn on your computer and hear whirring, crunching, or bumping sounds, turn it off immediately and don't turn it back on. Don't run any utilities. The sounds you are hearing are the heads hitting your disk. If you try to boot up, you'll lose all of your data. Contact your vendor or send the machine to a drive recovery facility.

GETTING HELP

Before you make a call, be sure to assemble the information you need. This may include the software version number, operating system, hardware you're using, equipment serial numbers, and contract numbers.

Call your help desk

If you're lucky, your company has a help desk, though many do not offer 24-hour, seven days a week service. If your problem occurs between 8 a.m. and 5 p.m., Monday through Friday, give your friendly help desk a call. The help desk staff may use a remote control program, such as Symantec's pcAnywhere, to take over your computer system and put it through its paces. They can run diagnostic programs, patch your software—even demonstrate procedures for you.

Contact your vendor

All software and hardware companies provide technical support for their products. There are a variety of ways to contact them.

■ **Telephone help**

Your company may have a special toll-free number or a contract number you'll need to obtain free support. If possible, call during the latter half of the week. Tech support staffs are most swamped on Mondays. Also, try to avoid late evenings when the help desk is on minimum staffing (that's also when they start the new trainees).

■ **Fax-back support**

With a fax machine or a fax modem, you can call a special number and order technical documents faxed to you immediately. Call to order an index first if you haven't used the fax-back system before.

Surf for answers

You'll find tons of technical information on online services and the Internet. Many software and hardware firms have Web pages that provide FAQs. Some super-sites have searchable databases of expert information. Microsoft has uploaded nearly 90 percent of its knowledge base (answers to technical questions written by the technicians themselves) onto the Web (*www.microsoft.com/support*). Another comprehensive site is Apple's Technical Information Library (*www.support.apple.com*). Healthy PC provides lots of free information, especially for the non-tekkie user (*www.zdnet.com/zdhelp/filters/healthypc*).

Some services will answer your e-mail requests for help. The Internet Help Desk (*http://w3.one.net/~alward*) is dedicated to everyone who has ever heard "I'm sorry, but we don't support that" from their friendly neighborhood help desk. The Geek Squad, a Minnesota-based group of technowizards, offers free cyberhelp as well (*www.geeksquad.com*).

Try an online fix

A variety of services help you tune up your system and avoid computer trouble:

■ Oil Change (*www.mcafee.com*) locates, downloads, and installs the latest upgrades and bug fixes for more than 6,500 programs.

■ Norton Web Services (*www.nortonweb.com*) locates and helps you install upgrades and hardware drivers you need to keep your system running well.

■ Intel's AnswerExpress (*www.intel.com*) provides live PC support via online access, virus protection, online backup, and an answer library.

■ Touchstone's CheckIt (*www.checkit.com*) provides diagnostic tools and crash recovery.

Use a user group

Software headaches getting you down? No one to turn to? Try contacting a local user group. Often composed of a group of volunteer experts, they arrange meetings, guest speakers, and demonstrations that help you get the most out of your software. To find out what organizations are active in your area, look in local computer publications, scan college and university bulletin boards, or check with your computer dealer.

Call a commercial helpline

Not every telecommuter has the luxury of an in-house help desk. And, even if you have one, it's probably not supported after hours or on weekends. So it's a good idea to have alternative help options available.

A good, though expensive, backup is a fee-based helpline. These services, often run 24 hours a day, are staffed by service reps trained to handle a multitude of problems. You might try the PC Crisis Line (800-828-4358).

Check with neighbors

Neighbors can be helpful too, as Keith Stefanczyk and his wife Dorice Exline discovered. As reported in *Arizona Republic Business*, the couple thought they were the only ones in their neighborhood who worked from home. "Then we saw all these Federal Express trucks and UPS delivery men cruising up and down the street all day," Stefanczyk observed. When they learned that more than half of their neighbors worked from home, they set up a network to help each other out. When Stefanczyk's fax machine went out suddenly, he just strolled next door and borrowed his neighbor's.

Another good way to meet telecommuting neighbors is at your local cafe or coffeehouse. Plan a visit in the late morning.

Locate the locals

Don't forget the corner copy shop, cybercafe, Kinko's, or Mailboxes Etc. These services can rent you equipment by the minute or by the hour to help you through the tough spots. Also, unless your company provides you with a loaner, you should find a good computer repair shop before you need it. Then, when the next emergency crops up, you'll be able to weather it like a pro.

Arrange for repair

There are times when you'll need to get your computer or peripheral fixed. Take it to the vendor's service center if the equipment is still under warranty. Your office may also specify a repair solution. However, if you own the equipment yourself and its warranty has expired, you'll probably need to make your own repair arrangements.

Radio Shack and Circuit City provide carry-in repair service for out-of-warranty computers and other equipment.

ESTABLISH REGULAR MAINTENANCE HABITS

Good computer health habits make a difference. Once you've lost a week's work in one blow, you'll know what I mean.

Make frequent backups

Make a partial backup at least daily. Make a complete backup of all your files and programs once a week. You'll be glad you did.

Invest in a tape backup or cartridge drive system if you have a large hard drive or need to back up a great number of files regularly. You'll save loads of time because you won't have to wait while the backup is being made or insert floppy after floppy. To shorten the task, use a file compression program such as StuffIt (*www.stuffit.com*) or PKZip (*www.pkware.com*). Better yet, backup to the Internet (see chapter 11 for more suggestions).

Clean up your act

Computer users come in a wide variety—some swear that tidy habits make their machines last longer; others (myself included) never clean anything unless it's broken. Well, almost never. I do clean the roller ball on my mouse from time to time with alcohol and a soft cloth. And, when I can't see the screen anymore, I wipe it down. That's it.

I share my office with two cats and there's lots of hair and dust around. Most experts suggest that I should dust the innards of my computer monthly to keep dust from forming on the computer's built-in fan. Otherwise, experts warn, dust buildup will cause the machine to overheat. The dusting job involves unscrewing the chassis and blasting the insides with a can of compressed air. Well, I never dusted any of my computer interiors and they've never broken. Maybe it's luck; maybe not.

But if you're a neatnik or a compulsive scrubber, you'll want to periodically clean the heads of your floppy-disk drive, vacuum your keyboard, dust your desk, and blow-dust your components with a can of compressed air.

Pay attention to temperature

Electronic equipment of all kinds—computers, cell phones, fax machines, printers, modems—can be harmed by extreme temperatures. If your office is hot, get air-conditioning. The equipment needs it more than you do.

When you travel and leave your equipment in the trunk of your car, pay particular attention to potential heat buildup. Park your car in the shade, use heat reflectors, or take the equipment with you.

Should you forget and your machine starts to fry, bring it indoors but don't open it up or try to use it. Let it come to room temperature naturally. Touch the screen periodically. When the screen feels the same temperature as the room, wait at least another hour before turning it on.

Cold can cause problems, too. Wiring shrinks and contacts can work loose when they get too cold. If you find your portable printer acting strangely, your laptop failing to wake up, or your cell phone refusing to dial, warm them up and try again. Some travel-savvy telecommuters carry a portable hair dryer for just such a purpose.

Hopefully, you won't have to go to the extremes that Mark Eppley did when climbing Washington's Mount Ranier. Eppley and his climbing pals planned to upload photos and dispatches of their trek onto the Internet and packed in loads of tech equipment. To keep keyboards and circuitry from freezing, the crew slept with their laptops snugged up against them in their sleeping bags. "I guess you'd call that the essence of workaholicism," Eppley laughed.

TROUBLESHOOTER'S TOOLKIT

The contents of your toolkit will vary, depending on your bravery quotient and the type of equipment you use. At the very least, you should have:

- Tiny screwdriver—for tightening printer and modem cables and other connections
- Miniflashlight—for peering into dark corners
- Small paintbrush—for cleaning fuzz, paper dust, and other electronic soot
- Tweezers or needlenose pliers—for fishing out bits of paper jammed in your printer

---

Note: *Jensen Tools* (www.jensentools.com) *makes a minikit filled with useful small tools for working with electronic equipment.*

Other handy items include:

- Bootable floppy disk—for starting up your system if your hard disk fails
- Utility programs—for restoring erased files, fixing bad disk sectors, and so on
- Extra cables—in case of a break
- Alligator clips—for hot-wiring phone lines
- A variety of adapters, line testers, splitters, and phone extension cords

FOR MORE INFORMATION

This book itself is loaded with troubleshooting tips. For more information, check out the following troubleshooting sections:

- Chapter 3—troubleshooting tips for corded and cordless phones
- Chapter 4—opening e-mail attachments, stopping spam
- Chapter 5—modem troubleshooting
- Chapter 6—faxing on the road, international faxing
- Chapter 9—making international connections, road warrior's survival kit
- Chapter 11—passwords, computer viruses, power problems, disasterproofing, espionage

RESOURCES

Books

Win 98 Optimizing & Troubleshooting Little Black Book
by Mark L. Chambers
The Coriolis Group, 1998

MacWorld Mac Upgrade and Repair Bible
by Todd Stauffer
IDG Books Worldwide, 1998

APPENDIX A

More Resources

BOOKS

■ Setting Up a Telecommuting Program

The Telecommuter's Handbook: How to Work for a Salary Without Ever Leaving the House, 2nd Edition
by Brad & Debra Schepp
McGraw-Hill, 1995
Packed with useful information for setting up a telecommuting relationship with your organization. Lists 50 jobs best suited for telecommuting and 100 companies with telecommuting programs.

An Organizational Guide to Telecommuting: Setting Up and Running a Successful Telecommuting Program
by George M. Piskurich
American Society for Training & Development, 1998
Presents a comprehensive evaluation of a telecommuting program and guidelines on how to implement a program. Considers the issues of selecting, training, and managing telecommuters. Includes samples of telecommuter evaluation forms.

■ Management Issues

Managing Telework: Strategies for Managing the Virtual Workplace
by Jack Nilles
John Wiley & Sons, 1998
The authoritative book on setting up a corporate telework program. Nilles coined the term "telecommuting" while stuck in a Los Angeles traffic jam.

Managing Virtual Teams: Practical Techniques for High-Technology Project Managers
by Martha Haywood
Artech House, 1998
Lots of good advice on developing distributed teams including building team identity, developing practical performance metrics, and mentoring and training remote workers. Includes an in-depth discussion of remote access technologies and more.

Telecommuting: A Manager's Guide to Flexible Work Arrangements
by Joel Kugelmass
Lexington Books, 1995
Written for managers responsible for evaluating and/or implementing flexible work arrangements.

Work Transformation: Planning and Implementing the New Workplace
by Henry Boehm
HNB Publishing, 1999
Contains several case studies including Waldorf Shared Telework Center, Hitachi America Limited, Northern Telecom's Corporate City, DEC's Space Sharing, Southern California Edison, and many more.

■ Flexible Work Arrangements

Breaking Out of 9 to 5: How to Redesign Your Job to Fit You
by Maria Laqueur & Donna Dickinson
Peterson's Guides, 1994
Includes information on flextime, job sharing, temping, permanent part-timing, telecommuting, compressed workweek, and self-employment.

■ Getting Organized

The Ultimate Home Office Survival Guide
by Sunny & Kim Baker
Peterson's Guides, 1998
Filled with tools, techniques, support systems, and procedures, this "full-time office consultant in book form" enables entrepreneurs and home-based corporate employees to establish routines and policies that work.

The Virtual Office Survival Handbook:
What Telecommuters and Entrepreneurs Need to Succeed in Today's Non-Traditional Workplace
by Alice Bredin
John Wiley & Sons, 1996
A comprehensive guide for surviving and thriving in a home office, mobile office, or any other nontraditional workplace.

■ Technology

Telecom Made Easy (3rd edition)
by June Langhoff
Aegis Publishing Group, 1997
A guide through the maze of telephone products and services, written in an easy-to-understand style. Subjects include: telephones, answering machines, fax, e-mail, Internet, online services, remote computing, cellular services, groupware, paging, wireless and remote communications, modems, telephone services, long-distance services, and voice mail.

Telecommuting
by Osman Eldib & Daniel Minoli
Artech House, 1995
A highly technical guide to telecommuting technology including networking solutions, CTI integration, and high-bandwidth communications.

■ Especially for Lawyers

Telecommuting for Lawyers
by Nicole Belson Goluboff
American Bar Association, 1998
Lawyer Nicole Goluboff addresses her book to both law firms and lawyers and covers such issues as submitting a proposal, developing policies, selecting telecommuters, training, budgeting, designing the monitoring process, and choosing tools.

■ Alternative Officing

New Workplaces for New Workstyles
by Marilyn Zelinsky
McGraw-Hill, 1998
A guide to designing alternative work environments, ranging from telecommuting to hoteling, virtual officing, videoconferencing, and teaming.

■ Work/Life Balance

Home Office Solutions: How to Balance Your Professional and Personal Lives While Working at Home
by Alice Bredin & Kirsten M. Lagatree
John Wiley & Sons, 1998
Conquer the psychological and work-management problems associated with having a home office. The authors discuss the many challenges home office workers face including isolation, stress, burnout, time management problems, family and relationship conflicts, depression, and procrastination.

MAGAZINES

Home Office Computing
Loads of useful articles to help home office folks solve computing problems.
www.smalloffice.com

Mobile Computing and Communications

The best magazine for road warriors—or anyone who has to work from more than one remote site. Regularly reviews mobile phones, pagers, laptops, handhelds, and other portable equipment.
www.mobilecomputing.com

Telecommute

Designed for today's flexible workplace, this is the only magazine specifically written with telecommuters in mind. It's packed with useful tips, hints, and strategies.
www.telecommutemagazine.com

NEWSLETTERS

Telecommuting Review

Gil Gordon Associates
www.gilgordon.com

A monthly newsletter directed primarily at employers. Includes case studies, technical advice, legal and regulatory developments, transportation issues, employee relations, and supervisory topics.

ASSOCIATIONS

Association for Commuter Transportation

1518 K Street, N.W., Suite 503
Washington, DC 20005
202-393-3497
Dedicated to serving the commuter-transportation industry and professionals with information meeting the needs of its corporate and individual members.

International Telework Association & Council (ITAC)

204 E. Street N.E.
Washington, DC 20002
202-547-6157
www.telecommute.org

A nonprofit organization that provides members with telecommuting and teleworking information, research, trends, and networking opportunities.

ONLINE SUPPORT

CompuServe

The *Working from Home Forum* has an active Telecommuting section. You can chat with other telecommuters and wannabes—and maybe even link up for a virtual job. In addition to a message-posting area, there is a library bursting with telecommuting resources. I'm the section leader in the telecommuting forum and look forward to welcoming you.

http://go.compuserve.com/WorkFromHome

The Mining Company

Provides advice regarding working at home and runs a weekly telecommuting chat room.

http://telecommuting.miningco.com

WEB SITES

There are loads of sites with telecommuting information. Here are my favorites:

Canadian Telework Association

www.ivc.ca

This comprehensive site provides loads of information about telecommuting up north. This site also runs a telework job-matching board.

European Telework Online

www.eto.org.uk

Links to more than 1,200 sites in Europe. Last time we looked, 28 countries and 15 languages were represented.

Gil Gordon Associates

www.gilgordon.com

Consultant Gil Gordon provides excerpts from his newsletter, *Telecommuting Review*; loads of answers to common questions in his FAQ file; an excellent resources and technology section; and a comprehensive listing of other telecommuting sites on the Internet.

International Telework Association & Council (ITAC)
www.telecommute.org

ITAC's home page provides a step-by-step tutorial on setting up a telework program. Plus pointers to recent articles on telecommuting and telework, a manager's discussion group, and a host of other useful resources.

June Langhoff's Telecommuting Resource Center
www.langhoff.com

You can find summaries of recent research, statistics, and surveys on my site. Plus guidelines on convincing your boss to let you telecommute, a handy bookstore, a worldwide calendar of telecommuting events, tips for road warriors, jokes about working at home, and more.

Smart Valley's Telecommuting Guide
www.svi.org/telework

This site allows users to download a PDF file of its excellent *Telecommuting Guide.* It also contains lots of useful FAQs and information. The Smart Valley project involved several Silicon Valley firms including 3Com, Hewlett-Packard, Silicon Graphics, Cisco, and Tandem.

BOOKLETS

Business Use of Your Home
IRS publication #587
This publication covers home office deductions and tax laws applicable to using part of your home for business purposes. 800-829-1040.

Aptitude Test

Successful telecommuters are disciplined self-starters who like to work solo. Take the survey below to measure your chances for success. The more checkmarks, the higher your score. Here goes...

❏ Are you well-organized and goal-oriented? At the very least, you'll want to brush up on time-management skills.

❏ Are you effective at controlling distractions? Family, neighbors, and pets will compete for your attention.

❏ Do you work well with a minimum of supervision?

❏ Are the social aspects of the office environment relatively unimportant to you?

❏ Are you an effective communicator? You'll need to be—most of your interaction will take place over phone or e-mail.

❏ Can you set aside an area of your home to be used exclusively as an office?

❏ Are you comfortable with the idea of working solo?

❏ Can you get along without office support systems and personnel? (No more copier, message-takers, or production assistants. No PC guru or network administrator at your beck and call.)

❏ Can you easily get along without in-office reference material (or arrange to get copies for home)?

APPENDIX C

Getting Started

HOW TO GET STARTED

If you don't currently telecommute, and want to convince your boss that it makes sense for your organization (and, of course, for you), do some research. Crunch the numbers and make a formal presentation, showing how telecommuting will save the organization money. Be sure to include cost/benefit figures.

Do some sleuthing to discover the following costs at your company:

■ **Cost per square foot of office space (ask the facilities manager).** If you can't get this information, you can use an industry average. ONCOR International does a yearly survey of major metropolitan areas. The 1998 figures ranged from a high of $43/s.f. (per year) in San Francisco to a low of $19 in Los Angeles. New York and Boston were both $41; Washington, DC, $37; Denver, $21; Atlanta and Dallas, $23.

■ **Average occupancy per square foot.** This may be difficult to discover, because your company may not measure actual usage. If you don't have actual figures, you could cite a study by Dr. Franklin Becker, a professor at Cornell University and co-author of the book *Workplace by Design*. Becker surveyed worker practices and determined that 70 percent of desks, offices, and workstations are unoccupied during a typical workday. This statistic alone usually makes bosses pay attention.

■ **Cost per square foot for parking space.** The national average is $600/year per car.

■ **Average size of an office space or cubicle at your company.** Management office space averages about 200 square feet; administrative cubicles average about 80 square feet.

With these figures, you can develop a simple telecommuting benefit analysis like the one below:

Productivity increased	$7,500
Absenteeism reduced	453
Office space saved	1,440
Parking space saved	40
Potential annual savings per employee	$9,633

Assumptions: *Figures are based on telecommuting 2 days/week, an annual salary of $50,000, productivity increase of 15%, absenteeism reduced by 10%, parking at $600/year reduced by 40%, and use of central office facilities of 120 square feet @ $30/square foot rent per year reduced by 40%.*

Note: *You'll probably need to add costs to this equation. Typical start-up costs for a telecommuter working at home include the installation of a second telephone line and annual phone usage costs, software licenses to allow work on a second computer, and access to a help-desk support system. Many companies supply a computer and modem as well. Be sure to factor in some training costs, too.*

CONVINCING YOUR BOSS

If your company already allows flexible work options such as telecommuting, it will be relatively easy to convince your supervisor to let you telecommute. The main issues will involve proving your reliability and the appropriateness of your job for distance working. However, if you're hoping to be the first telecommuter in your organization, you face a larger task. First, you have to convince the company that telecommuting makes business sense. Only then can you plead your own case. Here's a method that should work for you:

1. Drop occasional tidbits about telecommuting into your business conversation. For example, if you see an article about a competitor starting a telecommuting program, be sure to tell your supervisor about it.

2. Collect information about remote working. Be on the lookout for articles about companies in your area and/or those that compete with your company. Highlight important facts that you want to stand out and circulate them in the office.

3. In planning your campaign, make a list of the issues of most concern to your company. For example, if your group is short staffed and your company is finding it difficult to attract and keep employees, you'll want to stress hiring and retention issues. If your organization is growing rapidly and space is at a premium, stress facility savings.

4. Ask for a face-to-face meeting with your boss (or, if your company culture dictates, write a memo—see appendix D for an example). Tell your supervisor that you'd like to talk about a proposal for an alternative work arrangement.

5. At the meeting, explain that you want to telecommute in order to get more work done. This is important! Even if your reason is to spend more time with your new baby, reduce stress, or cut your commute time, do not mention personal reasons. Concentrate on what the company wants to achieve, not on your own needs.

Other strong telecommuting sales points:

- Not enough room in the office. Share offices to alleviate crowding.

- Spend more time with customers. The result: higher sales volume.

- Improve global team communications.

- Anything to do with improving the bottom line.

6. Make sure that your job has measurable objectives, such as pages proofed, lines of code written, sales calls accomplished, projects completed. If you lack such metrics, start to identify some.

Sample Telecommuting Proposal

Use this memo as a template and customize it to suit your particular situation. If you'll be presenting instead of writing, use it as the basis for your speaker's notes.

To: Boss
From: _____
Re: Telecommuting program proposal

Telecommuting is a widely accepted business practice and offers major advantages for organizations of all sizes. Cyber Dialogue, a New York-based research firm, surveyed the American workplace in 1998 and showed an estimated 15.7 million telecommuters, nearly 11 percent of the U.S. workforce. These ranks are growing at a rate of 20 percent a year. A number of our competitors, including _____ and _____ now offer telecommuting as a workplace option. [Insert names of business competitors that support telecommuting. If you don't know of any, check appendix E or my Web site (www.langhoff.com).] I've attached clippings from newspapers and magazines describing successful telecommuting results at other companies in our area.

Our company would benefit from the flexibility and productivity improvements telecommuting can offer. Specifically, we could experience:

■ Facility cost savings

Telecommuting frees up scarce resources such as office and parking lot space. Dr. Franklin Becker, a professor at Cornell University and co-author of *Workplace by Design*, surveyed worker practices and determined that 70 percent of desks, offices, and workstations are unoccupied during a typical workday. I know that's true of us. We've been suffering from cramped conditions here at the company headquarters for over a year.

By sharing offices, we can achieve important cost savings of approximately 120 square feet per office, not to mention reduced parking, water, heat, electricity, and office cleaning expenses. If we had just 20 telecommuters sharing 10 offices, we'd save _____ annually. [Find out how much your company pays for office space. Multiply the square foot cost per year by 10 and insert the dollar amount.]

AT&T saves an average of $3,000 per teleworker annually in real estate and associated costs. IBM saved $50 million annually and cut its U.S. real estate holdings by 22 million square feet. I've attached a cost-benefit analysis to highlight some of the savings we can anticipate.

■ Reduced sick leave

Telecommuters continue to work when a minor ailment might keep them away from the office. They actually work longer hours and more workdays than the average employee—exceeding them by one or two workdays a year. Our division averages ___ sick days a year. Cutting this by even a day results in annual savings of _____. According to the 1996 Unscheduled Absence Survey by CCH Inc., absenteeism costs $603 a year per employee. A 1998 survey by The Gallup Poll commissioned by CIGNA Integrated Care concluded that companies can add one or two points to their profit margin simply by reducing the average employee absentee rate by one day.

■ Productivity improvements

Telecommuters and their managers report that workers get more done when out of the office. In an AT&T-sponsored survey of Fortune 1000 managers, 58 percent reported increased worker productivity. Other studies show productivity gains ranging from 10 percent to 40 percent. This would translate into immediate bottom-line results for our company.

■ Improved hiring and retention

Demand for skilled information workers is at a high point, and the U.S. unemployment rate is at a quarter-century low. According to one recent study, one-third of companies with telecommuting programs use them as a lure to attract qualified employees. Our company spends a minimum of _____ in recruiting and training costs for each nonexempt employee hired, and turnover last year averaged _____. [If you don't have a figure for recruitment and training costs, use the industry average of $50,000.] According to telework consultant Gil Gordon, turnover conservatively costs 50 percent of annual salary. Any improvement in turnover is a win for us.

■ Improved contingency response

Our area was hit by a major ice storm in early 1998. Headquarters had to close for a day because employees were unable to get to work. [Replace this with a disaster story (earthquake, flood, hurricane, highway repairs, etc.) that affected your area.] Companies with teleworkers stay open when disaster strikes because the workers are able to conduct business from home.

■ Improved customer service

A number of organizations have reported that a distributed workforce results in additional sales and improved responsiveness to customers. Though it may be difficult to isolate the metrics, more face time with clients should have a positive impact on our revenues.

Here are suggested steps for implementing a program:

1. Start with a pilot program. I'd like to volunteer my department to test the program and work out any bugs. Our group would be appropriate because much of the work we do (budget analysis, project writing, and report drafting) could effectively be done off-site. Plus, we already have a work output performance measurement system in place.

2. Set up a multidisciplinary task force with representatives from Information Systems, Human Resources, Facilities, Legal, Finance, and Labor Relations. Our task would be to study best practices and develop specific policies.

3. Identify program costs and adjust budgets to fund adequately.

4. Develop standards for selecting telecommuters.

5. Begin an internal public relations campaign to sell managers and supervisors on the benefits of telecommuting. Process teleworker applications and select initial group.

6. Identify benchmarks to track the effect of telecommuting on the organization. We could track customer satisfaction rates, job-completion percentages, time required for particular tasks, expanded service hours, facility savings, sick leave costs, and turnover rates.

7. Provide training for telecommuters, their supervisors, and coworkers who will remain in the office.

8. Launch the trial. I suggest we give it at least six months.

9. Evaluate the program. This should take place at regular intervals and include focus groups and individual interviews. Thus, if any problems occur, they can be ironed out quickly.

I'm eager to prepare an in-depth proposal for the Executive Committee. Please let me know your thoughts.

your signature
contact info

Companies

COMPANIES WITH TELECOMMUTERS

This is a list of many of the corporations that have formal or informal telecommuting programs. My list was gleaned from magazines, online postings, newsletters, books, newspaper articles, and company press materials.

If your company is telecommuter-friendly and is not listed, let me know and I'll add it next time.

3Com	Century 21	Fleet Financial Group
Aetna Life Insurance	CH2M Hill	Ford Motor Company
Airtouch	Charles Schwab	Genentech
America West Airlines	Chevron	Georgia Power Company
American Airlines	CIGNA	GTE
American Express	CISCO Systems	Gymboree Corporation
Ameritech	Citibank	Hartford Insurance
Apple Computer	Coca-Cola	Herman Miller
Arthur Andersen	Compaq	Hewlett-Packard
AT&T	Control Data	Holland-America Westours
Autodesk	Corning	Honeywell
Bank of America	DEC	IBM
Banker's Trust	Deloitte and Touche	Intel
Bell Atlantic	Delta Airlines	J.C. Penney
Bellcore	Dun & Bradstreet	Jet Propulsion Laboratory
Best Western	E.I. Du Pont de	John Hancock Mutual Life
Black & Veatch	Nemours	Insurance
Blue Cross/Blue Shield	Eastman Kodak	Kaiser-Permanente
Boeing	EDS	Kraft General Foods
Borland International	Ernst & Young	Land's End
British Petroleum	Fenwick & West	

Lawrence Livermore
  Laboratories
Levi-Strauss
The Leisure Company
Lexis-Nexis
Lockheed Martin Missiles
  & Space
Lotus
Marriott International
McDonnel Douglas
MCIWorldCom
Merck & Co.
Merrill Lynch
MicroFocus
Mobil Oil
Motorola
Nationwide Insurance
NCR

New York Life Insurance
Nortel
Novell
Oracle
Pacific Bell
Patagonia
PeopleSoft
Perkin-Elmer
Pricewaterhouse
  Coopers Llp
Prudential
Sears Roebuck & Co.
Silicon Graphics
SkyTel
Sony Electronics
Southern California
  Edison
Sun Microsystems

Symantec
Tandem Computers
Texas Instruments
Toshiba
Travelers Insurance
Traveling Software
TRW
Union Pacific
Unisys
United Airlines
US West
VeriFone
Visa International
Wendy's
  International
Weyerhaeuser
Xerox
Zitel

Loads of federal, state, county, and city agencies have telecommuting programs. Here are just a few:

Cities:

Bloomfield, NB; Denver, CO; Glasgow, KY; Los Angeles, CA; Portland, OR; Redmond, WA

States:

Arizona, California, Colorado, Connecticut, Florida, Georgia, Hawaii, Massachusetts, Minnesota, New Jersey, Oregon, Utah, Virginia, Washington, Wisconsin

U.S. Federal Government:

Air Force, Commerce Department, General Services Administration, Environmental Protection Agency, Department of the Interior, Labor Department, NASA, Navy, Smithsonian Institution, Transportation Department, State Department

Countries:

Australia, Austria, Belgium, Bulgaria, Canada, Costa Rica, Crete, Czech Republic, Denmark, Finland, France, Germany, Greece, Hungary, Ireland, Israel, Italy, Latvia, Luxembourg, Japan, Norway, Netherlands, Poland, Portugal, Russia, Spain, Sweden, Switzerland, Ukraine, United Kingdom

Jobs

Jobs best-suited for telecommuting are those where a person often works alone. Since most telecommuters spend two to three days a week at their central office, it's easy to save project work, reading, report drafting, and research for the days at home. Days in the office are used for face-to-face meetings, team sessions, use of office equipment and resources, and the like.

I've been conducting an unofficial survey of the jobs held by telecommuters. Here's my list:

accountant	civil servant	detective
actor	claims processor	distance learning
actuary	clinical psychologist	instructor
administrator	collections agent	economist
advice nurse	college recruiter	editor
arbitrageur	columnist	engineer
architect	computer game designer	environmental analyst
artist	consultant	estate planner
astrologer	controller	estimator
auditor	copywriter	event planner
banker	court transcriber	explorer
booking agent	credit counselor	financial advisor
bookkeeper	customer service	fund-raiser
budget analyst	representative	grant writer
career counselor	data entry clerk	graphic artist
cartoonist	database administrator	human relations
CEO	designer	professional
city planner	desktop publisher	illustrator

importer
indexer
information broker
instructional designer
insurance agent
insurance claims adjuster
interpreter
interviewer
journalist
judge
laboratory scientist
lawyer
legal assistant
loan broker
maintenance technician
manager
market researcher
medical biller
medical transcriber
museum curator
musician
mutual fund manager
network manager
news reporter
nuclear engineer

office support
paralegal
patent searcher
personnel manager
political consultant
poll taker
private investigator
probation officer
professor
programmer
psychologist
public relations
   representative
purchasing agent
radio newscaster
radiologist
real estate agent
record producer
reporter
researcher
reservation agent
risk analyst
salesperson
scriptwriter
secretary

securities analyst
service technician
software engineer
sound mixer
   (engineer)
speechwriter
statistician
stockbroker
systems analyst
talent agent
tax preparer
teacher
technical writer
telemarketer
trainer
transcriber
translator
transportation analyst
travel agent
urban planner
virtual assistant
webmaster
word processor
workplace strategist
writer

Index

Other Books From Aegis Publishing Group

Available in bookstores or by calling 800-828-6961
(bulk purchases: 401-849-4200)

Winning Communications Strategies
*How Small Businesses Master Cutting-Edge Technology to Stay
Competitive, Provide Better Service and Make More Money*, by Jeffrey
Kagan
$14.95, ISBN: 0-9632790-8-4, paper, 219 pages, 5-1/2" x 8-1/2"

Find out how even the smallest companies are leveraging technology by
using powerful tools—such as fax-on-demand, voice mail, interactive
voice response, intranets, videoconferencing, and computer-telephony
integration—to stay ahead of their largest rivals.

Telecom Made Easy
*Money-Saving, Profit-Building Solutions for Home Businesses,
Telecommuters and Small Organizations*, by June Langhoff
$19.95, ISBN: 0-9632790-7-6, paper, 400 pages, 5-1/2" x 8-1/2"

More than 100,000 copies in print! The best basic telecom guide in
print. Find out how to benefit from the latest technology, from basic
wiring options and answering devices to ISDN and going online. Used
by telephone companies for training their own nontechnical sales and
customer service people, and as a premium for their business customers.

Telecom Business Opportunities
*The Entrepreneur's Guide to Making Money in the Telecommunications
Revolution*, by Steve Rosenbush
$24.95, ISBN: 1-890154-04-0, paper, 320 pages, 5-1/2" x 8-1/2"

This first-of-its-kind guide by *USA Today* telecom reporter Steve
Rosenbush shows where the money is to be made in the evolving,
deregulated telecommunications industry. Includes 20 fascinating
profiles of the entrepreneurs who are reshaping this enormous $750
billion global industry.

The Business Traveler's Survival Guide
How to Get Work Done While on the Road, by June Langhoff
$9.95, ISBN: 1-890154-03-2, paper, 128 pages, 5-1/2" x 8-1/2"

This handy guide covers the technology of how to stay connected on the road, including remote working, data security, groupware, teleconferencing, what to pack in the road warrior's tool kit, and international modem connections. Pack it on every business trip for ready reference.

1-800-Courtesy
Connecting With a Winning Telephone Image, by Terry Wildemann
$9.95, ISBN: 1-890154-07-5, paper, 144 pages, 5-1/2" x 8-1/2"

Much more than a book about telephone manners, *1-800-Courtesy* offers a unique and effective method for winning friends and influencing people over the telephone. Learn to identify verbal cues, project a positive attitude, and provide superior service.

The Telecommuter's Advisor
Real World Solutions for Remote Workers, 2nd edition, by June Langhoff
$14.95, ISBN: 1-890154-10-5, paper, 251 pages, 5-1/2" x 8-1/2"

Over 100,000 copies sold. The bible for remote workers who need help putting the latest technology to use in getting their work done while away from the office. Ideal for organization-wide telecommuting training and support programs.

900 KNOW-HOW
How to Succeed With Your Own 900 Number Business, 3rd edition, by Robert Mastin
$19.95, ISBN: 0-9632790-3-3, paper, 350 pages, 5-1/2" x 8-1/2"

Become a toll collector on the information highway. Learn the secrets to success in one of the most exciting new businesses spawned by the exploding information age. Launch a 900 number business and make money by the minute selling information 24 hours a day.

Telecom & Networking Glossary
Understanding Communications Technology, by Aegis Publishing Group
$9.95, ISBN: 1-890154-09-1, paper, 144 pages, 5-1/2" x 8-1/2"

Ever wonder what *asynchronous transfer mode* really means? Or how *ISDN* or *ADSL* can help your business? Or what *packet switching* is all about? This glossary of telecom and data networking terms will demystify the arcane language of telecommunications so that nontechnical end users will understand what it all means and how to put it to use to solve everyday business challenges.

Data Networking Made Easy
The Small Business Guide to Getting Wired for Success, by Karen Patten
$19.95, ISBN: 1-890154-15-6, paper, 250 pages, 5-1/2" x 8-1/2"

The smallest organizations will prosper by taking advantage of the latest networking technology. Electronic commerce and the Internet are the future, and even mom-and-pop businesses are using LANs and WANs to conduct business more efficiently. This book tells you how to get connected properly.

The Telecommunication Relay Service (TRS) Handbook
Empowering the Hearing and Speech Impaired, by Franklin H. Silverman, Ph.D.
$9.95, ISBN: 1-890154-08-3, paper, 128 pages, 5-1/2" x 8-1/2"

Telecommunication Relay Services (TRS) allow those who are hearing or speech impaired to communicate with anyone in the world. They can order a pizza, make a doctor's appointment, chat with a friend or discuss business with a client—common interactions the nonimpaired take for granted every day. This easy-to-read handbook will help both impaired and nonimpaired people communicate with one another for their mutual benefit.

Phone Company Services
Working Smarter with the Right Telecom Tools, by June Langhoff
$9.95, ISBN: 1-890154-01-6, paper, 102 pages, 5-1/2" x 8-1/2"

From Call Forwarding to Caller ID to 500 Service to ISDN to Centrex, this book describes phone company services in detail, and how to put them to their best use in real-life applications. This book clarifies the features and benefits of the myriad services available from phone companies, a subject that is getting more complex as the line between local and long-distance companies blurs.

Money-Making 900 Numbers
How Entrepreneurs Use the Telephone to Sell Information, by Carol Morse Ginsburg and Robert Mastin
$19.95, ISBN: 0-9632790-1-7, paper, 336 pages, 5-1/2" x 8-1/2"

Money gets made in this industry, but by whom? Here's the comprehensive guide to what programs have been tried, which ones are still around, and which ones didn't last. This book shows how imaginative entrepreneurs are using 900 numbers to sell information of all kinds over the telephone. From the mundane to the exotic, nearly 400 real-life programs covering every possible application are profiled.

The Cell Phone Handbook
Everything You Wanted to Know About Wireless Telephony (But Didn't Know Who or What to Ask), by Penelope Stetz
$14.95, ISBN: 1-890154-12-1, paper, 336 pages, 5-1/2" x 8-1/2"

Cellular phones have gone from a *gee whiz* curiosity to an indispensable communications link for more than 70 million U.S. subscribers. Despite cell phones' enormous popularity, it has been difficult to get reliable, objective information on which to base purchases and maximize performance. Until now. This book gives you a solid understanding of wireless technologies so you can make an informed purchase decision the next time you buy wireless equipment or services.

How to Buy the Best Phone System
Getting Maximum Value Without Spending a Fortune, Sondra Liburd Jordan
$9.95, ISBN: 1-890154-06-7, paper, 136 pages, 5-1/2" x 8-1/2"

Small businesses are faced with a confusing array of choices in purchasing the company's most vitally important business tool: the communications system that interacts with the outside world and gives that all-important first impression to callers. A phone system can either facilitate or impede smooth communications, and the difference can make or break a small business. This straightforward book will help the busy, nontechnical manager make the right choice.

Getting the Most From Your Yellow Pages Advertising
Maximum Profits at Minimum Cost, 2nd edition, by Barry Maher
$19.95, ISBN: 1-890154-05-9, paper, 304 pages, 5-1/2" x 8-1/2"

The perennial bible on the subject. Learn how to get the most mileage out of your advertising dollars, increasing sales as cost-effectively as possible. Learn what kinds of ads pull the best response, and how to avoid common money-wasting mistakes. Invest your advertising dollars as wisely as possible and watch your sales soar.

Digital Convergence
How the Merging of Computers, Communications, and Multimedia Is Transforming Our Lives, by Andy Covell
$14.95, ISBN: 1-890154-16-4, paper, 240 pages, 5-1/2" x 8-1/2"

The tools of human interaction—images, video, sound, and text—can now be defined and represented digitally. This common digital format—where virtually everything is represented by 1s and 0s—allows information to be transmitted, stored, combined, and manipulated in ingenious ways that are still being discovered and perfected. The World Wide Web, videoconferencing, e-mail, groupware, Internet telephony, and digital television are only the earliest examples of new technologies spawned by digital convergence.

Strategic Marketing in Telecommunications
How to Win Customers, Eliminate Churn, and Increase Profits in the Telecom Marketplace, by Maureen Rhemann
$39.95, ISBN: 1-890154-17-2, paper, 320 pages, 5-1/2" x 8-1/2"

The telecommunications industry is undergoing unprecedented upheaval as the world deregulates and monopolies break apart. This book offers telecom professionals up-to-the-minute guidance on how to tackle the tough marketing issues that face them. They will learn what is working and not working for other companies in the industry, and they will find solutions to the unique challenges of the telecom industry.